GOD
Can Use

Remarkable Stories of Ordinary Christians

Little Ole
ME

GOD
Can Use

Remarkable Stories of Ordinary Christians

Randy Clark

Revival Press

An Imprint of
Destiny Image® Publishers, Inc.
P.O. Box 310
Shippensburg, PA 17257-0310

ISBN 1-56043-696-4

For Worldwide Distribution
Printed in the U.S.A.

First Printing: 1998   Second Printing: 1998

This book and all other Destiny Image, Revival Press,
and Treasure House books are available
at Christian bookstores and distributors worldwide.

For a U.S. bookstore nearest you, call **1-800-722-6774**.
For more information on foreign distributors, call **717-532-3040**.
Or reach us on the Internet: **http://www.reapernet.com**

Endorsements

Did you ever wonder if God would use you to do something awesome, or even just a little out of the ordinary, for Him? Many preachers are saying that we must release the people in the pew, but Randy is not just preaching it; he is *doing* it. Randy Clark knows how you feel. He really is a "little ole me" who has simply stepped out in faith to be powerfully used by the Lord. There is a growing number of ordinary people who are doing extraordinary things for God. You are probably one of those people. I recommend that you read this book—there is no telling what you might find yourself doing for the Lord!

Don Nori, Publisher
Destiny Image Publishers

I met Randy Clark for the first time with some reservations in mind. At that time, his connection with the move of the Spirit that came to be known as the "Toronto Blessing" created a lot of trouble for me. However, after three hours of personal and in-depth conversation, I came to realize that he was an honest servant of God. That change of attitude on my part released opportunities for me to enjoy serving the Lord together with Randy on various occasions. How much I have learned from him! How true it is that God can use little servants like us. I'm sure that most readers will be inspired by Randy's message in this book, and will be encouraged to let the Lord use their lives for great things.

Dr. Pablo A. Deiros, Senior Pastor
Del Centro Evangelical Baptist Church, Argentina

Randy Clark's book, *God Can Use Little Ole Me*, is a refreshing drink of water for the soul. He writes in a humorous style that is down-to-earth, yet heavenly inspired. For all those who are thirsty for a deep touch of the Lord's Presence, this book is a must-read.

Cindy Jacobs, Co-Founder
Generals of Intercession

This is a *must* for every Christian who wants more of God! It is a timely word for God's people as we sense the mobilizing stir of the Holy Spirit in these days. This book will stir you and give you new hope to allow the Holy Spirit to channel His awesome power through *you*! As Randy Clark shares and reveals his heart in a down-to-earth fashion, I believe many Christians who long for reality with God will be encouraged and motivated as they realize that "God can use little ole me!"

François Van Niekerk, Senior Pastor
Hatfield Christian Church North, South Africa

This happy book presents a simple and gladdening proposition—that God can use any of us. Randy is the first to admit that, as men go, he was among the most unlikely to be used to spark a raging fire of renewal. Yet, today, under the auspices of his simple organization, the title of which contains the word *global*, his ministry touches the continents of the whole earth. The question comes to us all again and again: "Can God...?" In this book, on page after page, the answer comes again and again in the unarguable results of changed lives, "Yes, He can use, has used, and is using the little ole me's of our day!"

Jack Taylor
Dimensions Ministries

As Randy Clark shares his testimony and those of others involved in the current outpouring of the Holy Spirit, you will be encouraged and excited at how God suddenly transported them from skepticism, despair, and dryness to active participation. With great clarity and refreshing transparency, Randy lets us get an inside glimpse into the lives of those God is using to ignite His flames of revival throughout the world. You will be inspired to believe that God can and will use you.

Dutch Sheets, Pastor
Springs Harvest Fellowship

Many people do not really believe that they have a significant and unique contribution to make in God's Kingdom. Therefore, Randy's book is a timely message for ordinary people who may need encouragement that they can be used by an extraordinary God. He tells his own story, reinforced with the stories of many others, and makes this point clear and exciting. In a candid, ordinary, yet effective style—characteristic of Randy—*God Can Use Little Ole Me* will warm the hearts and motivate the actions of all who read it.

Roger Helland, Senior Pastor
New Life Vineyard Fellowship, Canada

Randy Clark is one of the most normal, yet spiritual, men I know. His life and ministry is a testimony to the compassionate, healing power of Jesus that is oftentimes poured through vessels of clay. The book, *God Can Use Little Ole Me*, is a shining example of Randy's heart to see the sick and hurting healed, and to encourage all believers that they too can "do the works of Christ."

Larry Randolph
Larry Randolph Ministries

Randy Clark is not only an educated theologian, but also one of the nicest and most humble men I know in the ministry. He is a fire-lighter in the Kingdom of God to whom all of us impacted by the "Toronto Blessing" owe a huge debt of gratitude. I enthusiastically recommend *God Can Use Little Ole Me*.

John Arnott, Senior Pastor
Toronto Airport Christian Fellowship, Canada

I have often heard it said and preached that God has no favorites but, in fact, we see through the Scriptures that God sovereignly shows grace and favor to those who obey Him. God chose Randy Clark for this last-day great move of God and I believe He did so because Randy really believes "God can use little ole me." That is the key, the secret of his success—always has been, always will be.

John Kilpatrick, Pastor
Brownsville Assembly of God

Contents

Foreword

Randy Clark's book is largely a collection of true stories of "ordinary" people doing extraordinary things. Randy dispels the myth that only high profile Christians or leaders see unusual things happen in their own experiences. Indeed, the most ordinary men and women become sovereign vessels of God when they are obedient.

Randy was utterly surprised when he began to see himself used so powerfully, but what amazed him even more was the fact that the people he touched through the laying on of hands ended up doing even more astonishing things! That is what this book is about.

I have met Randy Clark only once. I went out of my way to hear him and meet him. I knew him to be the "link" between the ministry of Rodney Howard-Browne and the "Toronto Blessing," as it came to be called. I wanted to meet this man whose trip to Toronto unexpectedly made the world take note of God's unusual manifestation there. The upshot was that this fire spread around the world.

Surprisingly, Randy tells very little of what happened when Rodney Howard-Browne prayed for him. I have heard both sides of the story—from Randy and Rodney. What happened was this. After being prayed for a number of times by Rodney, with apparently nothing happening, suddenly Randy exclaimed, "My hands are frozen!" Rodney replied, "That's the fire of God—lay hands on anything that moves!" Randy began doing that; Toronto was only the beginning about two weeks later.

It is my own conviction that the need of the day is for a coming together of the Word and the Spirit. There has been, sadly, a silent divorce in the Church between the Word and the Spirit. In a divorce, some children stay with the mother; some stay with the father. In the Church today, this divorce has resulted in some staying on the "Word" side, and some on the "Spirit" side.

Let me explain. There are those who say, "The need of the hour is to return to the Word—to the faith once delivered to the saints. We need to get back to the God of the Reformation, the God of Luther, Calvin, Edwards, Whitefield. We must return to preaching, to the preaching of the gospel, the sovereignty of God, justification by faith." What is wrong with this emphasis? Absolutely nothing.

On the other side there are those who say, "The need of the hour is for a demonstration of signs, wonders, miracles. What will shake the nations and the Church is a manifestation of the gifts of the Spirit, the prophetic, the word of knowledge, healing. Until people see that God is the same as in the Book of Acts, they will remain unchanged." What is wrong with this emphasis? Absolutely nothing.

The emphasis on both sides, then, is absolutely right. But what is needed is for a remarriage of the Word and the Spirit—a coming together of the two. The simultaneous combination will mean spontaneous combustion. It is my view that the coalescence of the Word and the Spirit will result in the great revival that is needed.

Why do I write this Foreword? I come from the "Word" side of this silent divorce. But I am open to the Spirit. I prove this partly by urging those who identify with my own perspective to read this book. It will seem like an alien world to some. I don't claim to understand all I read, neither do I grasp the way God apparently touches some who are so far removed, historically, from the mainstream of the Evangelical wing of the Church. But Randy didn't make up these stories. They show how God crosses not only ecclesiastical but also theological boundaries—not unlike the situation the early Church faced in Acts 15.

It is humbling for me to accept—to this day—how God uses people whose theology isn't up to my "standard." But He continues to defy the sophisticated and still chooses the foolish things of the world to confound the wise (see 1 Cor. 1:27). I therefore urge that the reader develop an openness to the Holy Spirit in a manner heretofore thought unnecessary.

Randy Clark and I have several things in common. We are both American, we were both trained at Southern Baptist Theological Seminary in Louisville, Kentucky, and we both speak with a southern accent! What impresses me most about Randy, however, is his unpretentiousness. He is transparent.

It is my prayer that this book not only blesses those who are already at home with the kind of things described here, but that it will also create a hunger and thirst for more of God that those of us on the Word side, if we are honest, desperately need.

Dr. R.T. Kendall
Westminster Chapel, London

Chapter 1

A Thirsty Man

By the summer of 1993 I was on the verge of a nervous breakdown. The effects of 23 years of heartbreakingly difficult pastoral ministry were catching up with me. I had been sheep-bitten once too often and was incredibly weary from the constant labor of trying to build and grow a church during dry times. A critical glance, a cross word, or anything that even hinted at conflict was enough to make my chest muscles shake uncontrollably and my voice to tremble and break as my nerves gave way.

I had planted a Vineyard church in St. Louis, Missouri, in 1986 and in seven years had seen it grow to about 300 people. It had not been easy. After the first 11 months I had only 11 people. Perhaps that is not too bad for starting a church from scratch, and even 300 in seven years might be impressive to some. I was disappointed and discouraged, though, because I had come to St. Louis eagerly anticipating much more.

Prior to 1986 I was moving up the denominational ladder as a Baptist. I was a graduate of a Baptist seminary in Louisville, Kentucky, and pastored an American Baptist church in southern Illinois. In fact, the year I resigned (1984) was the year my Baptist church had won the evangelism award out of 250 American Baptist churches in Illinois and Missouri—a recognition given to only one church each year. The pastor of the church so honored was poised to advance in the denomination. I even had a pretty good salary. However, I walked away from it all because I was thirsty for more of God and wanted to emphasize that God still heals today, that He still delivers today, and that He wants to empower us today. I felt that the only way I could do that without splitting the church was to resign.

I had received a fresh baptism in the Holy Spirit in March 1984 (I had first received the baptism of the Holy Spirit in 1971) and ever since had been seeing God come in power with healing and deliverance. I conducted healing seminars at a number of different churches where God showed up; people were slain in the Spirit, healings occurred, and other miraculous things happened. It was an exciting time.

In the midst of this atmosphere of God's strong Presence I felt Him leading me to start the church in St. Louis. I was excited to go because I fully expected all the signs, wonders, and other evidence of God's Presence and power to continue. I took a job frying donuts, and after 11 months of commuting 300 miles round-trip every weekend planting the church, I was finally able to move my family to St. Louis. Church planting was exhausting, and only occasional refreshing visitations from God kept me from totally losing it.

During that first year we saw some healings and as we gathered people I trained a ministry team. At that time my idea of church growth was signs, wonders, healings, baptisms in the Spirit, deliverances, and words of knowledge. These things would then lead people to repentance and conversion. That first year was also the beginning of the desert. From 1986 to the fall of 1993 there was a general dryness in the Church at large, but I didn't know it for a long time. My nose was to the grindstone and I thought it was just my church and my ministry. I thought I was a failure. What had happened to God? Where did He go?

It was painful to be a pastor in dryness when nothing seemed to be happening. Our church believed in healing; we had a theology for it and we practiced it. We had a ministry team. We had words of knowledge. In the early days God's anointing was strong and we saw some good things happen in healing and deliverance. When the dry times hit, however, the anointing lifted and for years we saw almost no healings, deliverances, or other evidences of the strong Presence of God.

During this time I made an unconscious decision. Earlier I had heard John Wimber, the leader of the Vineyard movement, say that we needed to pay whatever price was necessary to stay in the fullness of the Spirit before God. I didn't pay it. It was easier to settle for external measures of success: buildings, baptisms, and budgets. I found out that most people preferred comfort to anointing.

So instead of turning to God and crying out desperately to Him in prayer, I measured the success of my ministry by comparing it to that of a friend who pastored a Vineyard church in another state. I tried to be like him and was instead dying inside. I reached the point where I wanted to quit the ministry altogether. I complained to God that I didn't like the church anymore. In my mind I heard Him say, "That's because it is too much you and not enough Me. For years you have built this church on your labor and your work, and it's killing you."

Somewhere along the line I had lost my perspective. Instead of building a church I had drawn a crowd. We had a lot of people but there was no anointing, no real spiritual power in their lives. I remember thinking, *God, if I can't have You in our midst, then I don't want to pastor. What's happened to me? I used to believe and teach signs and wonders and now I don't even expect them myself.* I knew that I had been born into the Charismatic movement in power, but when the power lifted, rather than cry out and thirst for more I unconsciously fell into the trap of looking for success in all the wrong places.

Finally, in the summer of 1993, I made the conscious decision to go back and pursue God. I didn't even care if half the church left in the process. I really had no other choice. I was at the end of my rope. I was dry and thirsty and had to rediscover the power, the anointing, and the Presence of God I had once known. If I didn't, I was finished in the ministry.

"You can lead a horse to water..."

> *On the last and greatest day of the Feast, Jesus stood and said in a loud voice, "If anyone is thirsty, let him come to Me and drink. Whoever believes in Me, as the Scripture has said, streams of living water will flow from within him." By this He meant the Spirit, whom those who believed in Him were later to receive. Up to that time the Spirit had not been given, since Jesus had not yet been glorified* (John 7:37-39).

According to these verses the Holy Spirit could not come until after Jesus was glorified. By "glorified" John means that Jesus had to be lifted up on the cross, lifted up in the resurrection, and lifted up in the ascension to the right hand of the Father. Jesus' glorification involved all three. Only then could the Spirit descend to fill and baptize and be an abiding presence in the lives of believers.

Jesus gives only one condition necessary for receiving the Spirit: thirst. Isn't it good that He didn't say we had to be smart or rich or be overcomers first? All we have to be is thirsty. When we are filled with the Spirit we become overcomers; it is a work of the Spirit. That is the meaning of grace. The other religions of the world say that we must become overcomers, that we must strive to reach God, and then we will be filled or engulfed in whatever spirit they worship. They have a philosophy of works. Jesus said that the Holy Spirit is a gift from God freely given to anyone who is thirsty.

> *For we were all baptized by one Spirit into one body—whether Jews or Greeks, slave or free—and we were all given the one Spirit to drink* (1 Corinthians 12:13).

This is a favorite verse for many who grew up in historic denominations because it emphasizes that all believers have been baptized by the Spirit, and that's where it ends for many of them. Notice what else Paul says, though: "...and we were all given the one Spirit to *drink*." What does it mean to drink of the Spirit? It means realizing we're thirsty, coming to God believing that He will pour out His water, His Spirit, and when He does, not running away afraid.

I'm sure we've all heard the old saying, "You can lead a horse to water but you can't make him drink." You can come to church and never drink. You can go to revival meetings and never drink. Drinking is a conscious act of the will. We choose whether or not to drink. How long has it been since you took a drink?

He said to me: "It is done. I am the Alpha and the Omega, the Beginning and the End. To him who is thirsty I will give to drink without cost from the spring of the water of life" (Revelation 21:6).

There's that word *thirsty* again. The water of life is *free* to anyone who is thirsty. That's a poetic way of saying it is by grace. We don't have to work for it and we can't buy it. Paul reminds us in First Corinthians 6:19-20 that we are not our own but were bought with a price, the blood of Jesus, and are therefore to glorify Him with our bodies. Jesus bought with His blood the life that He offers to us *without cost*. All we have to do is be thirsty.

When we are dry, we are not saturated with the presence of Jesus; our character is not characterized by the life of Jesus; and the fruit of the Spirit is not growing in us. When we drink from *the spring of the water of life*, it waters and nourishes the spiritual fruit in us: love, joy, peace, patience, kindness, goodness, faithfulness, gentleness, and self-control (see Gal. 5:22-23). At the same time it washes out the works of the flesh: fits of anger, jealousy, envy, violence, orgies, and such. The result is the growth of the presence of the Lord's character in our lives.

Several years ago I heard Paul Cain say that we have as much of God as we want. I didn't like that. I knew I wanted more of God than I had. So what did that statement say about me? The more I thought about it, however, the more I realized he was right. It is one thing to have only a slight desire for God, and quite another to be so thirsty for Him that nothing is more important than getting filled.

Sometimes God has to break through the parched dryness of our souls before He can refresh us with the river of His Spirit. Realizing that we're dry is not the same thing as wanting to be watered. God fills us according to our thirst. The thirstier we are when we come to Him, the more He fills us. How thirsty are you?

God on the Telephone

One night in that summer of 1993 God called me on the telephone. The call came through a friend I hadn't seen in nine years and who had been in my Baptist church when the Spirit fell in 1984. It was about midnight when I answered the phone.

"Randy, this is Jeff. How are you doing? How is the church?"

Now, there are two questions you should never ask a pastor: how he is doing and how his church is doing. Why? Because no matter what the truth may be, we pastors feel we have to put on our "preacher face" and say that everything is fine even when we are dying inside. Then later on we have to go repent of the lie. So save us the anguish and don't ask.

Jeff asked anyway, so in proper preacher fashion I answered, "Fine."

Then he said, "I'm glad you are doing great but I want you to know I've been doing terrible." He went on to remind me of what it had been like for us when the Spirit had fallen nine years earlier. Since then he had gone through dry times and was desperate for God to touch him. He was burned-out, tired, and used up. He had backslidden so badly that just a few weeks before he had been so close to suicide that he was sitting up at 3:00 a.m. with a pistol on the coffee table in front of him. He felt abandoned and forgotten by God.

Jeff told me that later that morning he got a call from a pastor friend who said that God had awakened him at 3:00 a.m. with a burden to intercede for Jeff against a spirit of suicide that was attacking him. He had prayed for several hours until the burden lifted. A little while later Jeff's aunt called asking about him because God had also roused her from sleep at 3:00 a.m. with a burden to pray for him.

Then Jeff said, "Randy, all of a sudden I knew God hadn't forgotten me." He said he knew those were phone calls from God.

I realized at that moment that Jeff's call too was a phone call from God. His questions had made me recognize that I was not doing fine and neither was my church. He had reminded me of the former days when I had seen the glory and power of God. Tears began running down my cheeks because I knew this was not a coincidental phone call. God had not forgotten me and He was coming to help.

Jeff said that sometime later he had gone into a convenience store and happened to pick up a copy of *Charisma* magazine, which he hadn't read in years. On the back was an invitation to a "signs and wonders" camp meeting with Dr. Rodney Howard-Browne in Louisville, Kentucky, in June 1993. Jeff had attended the meetings and had seen some bizarre things, such as people falling down all over, people laughing, and people getting "frozen" and remaining motionless for long periods of time.

Now, I had seen people fall before and I had seen some people laugh in church, so that wasn't enough to challenge me. I probably would not have gone to hear an evangelist just because people fell or laughed. I asked Jeff, "What's the bottom line? How has your life been different since you came back?"

He said, "Randy, I have seen more healings in the last two weeks than in the previous eight years combined."

God hooked me right then and there and began reeling in the line because He knew my heart was to see people healed. I told Jeff I would go to some of Rodney Howard-Browne's meetings, but I didn't follow up on it right away. Jeff called me every day, urging me on until finally I called and spoke to Dr. Howard-Browne's secretary.

Here was a ray of hope, and yet still I wondered what I might be getting into.

A Divine Setup

One thing I had always liked about the Vineyard movement was the emphasis placed on loving *all* of God's Church, from the litergical "high churches" (Orthodox, Anglican, Roman Catholic) to the Pentecostals, and everyone in between. I agreed with that idea and really did love the Church. There was one group, however, that I had a real problem with: the Word of Faith people. I had seen a particularly rabid and radical group of faith camp people in southern Illinois, and I had no use for the "name it and claim it, blab it and grab it, confess it and possess it" theology. I think part of my difficulty with faith camp people was because I had so little faith myself. I had reached a point where I didn't really expect very much from God.

God has a sense of humor though, and likes to set us up so He can work on our weaknesses. When I called Rodney Howard-Browne's office and asked where he would be during the week I was able to go, I found out that he would be at Kenneth Hagin's Rhema Bible Church in Tulsa, Oklahoma. I thought, *Oh, my God, the very center, the very Mecca and Medina of the faith camp!* God was testing my resolve. He wanted to see how serious I was for Him.

I knew Jeff's phone call had been God's wake-up call to me. Jeff had told me that Rodney Howard-Browne had said that a thousand men who would be prayed for at his meetings would then go out and do the same thing. That night I had sat up until 3:00 a.m. crying. I said, "Lord, I want to be one of those thousand. I'll do anything. I'll pay any price, just let me be used." I didn't really expect it to happen, though; my faith was too small. Now God was testing me, sending me into the very heart of the faith camp. It's as though He was saying to me, "How thirsty are you really for Me?"

Was it a coincidence? I knew better than that. This was no accident. God knew what He was doing all along. He set me up. That day I developed a greater appreciation for Naaman in Second Kings 5:1-14 who was told by the prophet Elisha to dip seven times in the Jordan River to be cleansed of his leprosy. At first Naaman balked. "Why don't we dip in our own river? Why do we have to go dip in this river?" When he obeyed, however, he was healed. The Lord said to me, "Are you thirsty enough for Me to do whatever I require in order to be filled?"

I was thirsty, so I went to Tulsa along with three other men from the church. I was so desperate for God that I had told my wife earlier that I would not eat again until God touched me. This scared her because she did not think God was going to touch me.

I was not impressed by the first meeting. Although I liked Rodney and his teaching, I was distracted by a woman on the main floor below me who laughed loudly and slowly throughout the meeting with a laugh that sounded as fake as anything I had ever heard. She annoyed me. Then I got annoyed at the ushers for not removing her. Finally I even got annoyed at Rodney for not doing anything. My attitude was rotten and I didn't get anything out of the first service.

During the next service Rodney talked about the laughing. He said that anyone who was laughing in the flesh could be removed and would be if it was appropriate. He went on to say, however, that people who laugh in the flesh often do so because they are hurt, wounded, and needing attention. Then he addressed those who get mad at the laughers. He said, "I want you to know that their flesh does not stink in God's nostrils nearly as much as your pharisaical judgment of them." After I took the Holy Spirit's knife of conviction out of my back and sat up again, God really had my attention.

The turning point for me came during the prayer and ministry time. Many people came forward to receive prayer, but the most credible witness to me was a blind boy who was brought forward. He couldn't have been more than two or three years old. When he received prayer he went out under the Spirit and lay still for a long time. I looked at my watch and back at the little boy, then back at my watch. Having four of my own, I understand children. At that time I had a one-year-old and a three-year-old. Children that age do not lie still on their own for anyone for as long as the little blind boy lay there. I knew this had to be God. For me, it was like the parting of the Red Sea. All of a sudden the meeting I had been judging judged me. In that instant I went from a detached, analytical observer to a desperately thirsty man. *Please, God*, I prayed, *please touch me. Please give me the chance to be prayed for.*

Thirst Quenched

Rodney didn't pray for everybody, and he didn't have anyone helping him either. He asked for only those who felt the anointing to come forward for prayer. He didn't want anyone to come up who didn't feel the anointing: a tingling sensation in the hands or on the head. I sat there and prayed, *Please, God, touch me. Give me a chance to go up.* Nothing happened—no tingling sensation or anything else. I left the meeting feeling frustrated.

The next morning I came back and sat as close to the front as possible. During the ministry time my associate pastor went forward, received prayer, and fell out under the Spirit. For me there was nothing. I came back the next night. By this time I was really getting desperate. There were only a couple of sessions left. I prayed, *Lord, give me something, anything, even just the air conditioner blowing over me! That will be enough! I really want to be touched.* To this day I don't know if it was my desperation or what, but I did feel my hand tingle a little bit. It was all I needed! I jumped up and got in line. Rodney came by and said, "Fill."

I had received a fresh baptism by the Spirit in 1984 while I was still a Baptist pastor. The Spirit had touched me in a powerful way again in 1989. Both times it felt like a surge of electricity went through my body, with the 1989 experience so strong that I literally thought it was going to kill me. The first time, in my Baptist church, I literally shook as I moved my feet to keep from falling to the floor. That's what being touched by the Spirit meant to me: electricity. That was my experience.

When Rodney touched me and said "Fill," I went down and lay there waiting for the electricity. Where was it? I didn't feel anything. *This isn't God*, I decided, *just psychological suggestion, and I'm weak-minded. I'm getting up.* I discovered then that I couldn't move. *Maybe this is God.* About that time the laughing started. It bubbled up from inside me and I couldn't stop. That was one of only three times I have ever been inebriated on the Spirit of God. Two weeks had passed since I had vowed not to eat until God touched me.

We came back the next day, the last session I could attend. That morning Rodney said he wanted to pray for anyone who wanted prayer. Despite my experience of the day before, I was still looking for the electricity. When the prayer time came I got in line. It seemed like all 4,500 people there wanted prayer. I hate lines. If I'm considering a certain restaurant for dinner and see more than 10 or 15 people in line, I go somewhere else. Nevertheless, I stayed in line while Rodney—one man, no ministry team—made his way to each person saying, "Fill, fill, fill." It must have been 45 minutes before he got to me. I went down and lay on the floor, but still there was no electricity. Rodney had said that you don't get drunk on a single drink, and I wanted to get as much as I could get. I got up and ran to another area of the building and got in line there. I got in line five times that day, and each time I was prayed for I went down, but I never felt any electricity.

At one point I was walking through the building looking at the nice, neat orderly lines of people lying on the floor and it reminded me of the scene in *Gone With the Wind* when Scarlett O'Hara walks among the rows and rows of wounded in Atlanta. As I looked around I said, "God, don't ever let me forget this; put this mental picture forever in my mind. God, I want to do this; I really want You to use me. I don't just want a blessing; I want You to bless me to be a blesser. Give me an anointing to minister to the needs of my people. Let me be one of the thousand." I still didn't believe that it would happen.

Sharing the Water

I returned from the meetings honestly wondering if anything had really happened to me. My associate pastor couldn't wait to see all this happen in our church, but I was more cautious. I felt I needed six months to teach the people on the Holy Spirit and prepare them for the experience. But the Holy Spirit had His own timetable.

In the eight years the church had been in existence, not one person had fallen out in the Spirit on a Sunday morning. The first Sunday back I made the mistake of asking the men who had gone with me to share their testimonies. After that, we began to worship. We had barely begun to sing when a woman who was a member of the wealthiest and most prestigious family in our church suddenly fell out in the Spirit, laughing. Just before being hit with laughter and falling to the floor, she had seen the "shekinah glory cloud" roll into the back of the church. She was on the floor for 45 minutes. I invited anyone who wanted to, to come forward for prayer. Many responded, lining up from wall to wall. Now, I was used to a low-grade anointing: pray for 20 minutes and maybe a left eyelid will flutter. That was about it. That Sunday was different. I touched one woman; boom, she went down. I touched another person; boom. I thought I had died and gone to Heaven. Boom, boom, boom. It was a preacher's dream. It was so much fun and I had a great time. We had people out for four hours. Lives were changed that day.

One young man there that morning, a law school graduate, was not impressed. In fact, he was mad at me. He thought it was all psychological suggestion and that I had set it up. Just prior to the invitation, he had come forward for communion and was standing at the end of the line of people I was praying for. I thought he was waiting for prayer. Before I could pray for him, he said, "I don't believe this is real."

Puzzled, I asked him, "If you don't believe this is real, then why are you in line?"

"I'm not in line."

"Why are you standing here then?"

"I can't move."

Here was a skeptic, critical of what he saw happening around him, yet frozen by the Spirit and unable to move! He had stood up to leave the communion rail and found himself rooted to the spot.

I said, "It looks like you're not going anywhere. Why don't you let me pray for you?" He conceded.

As soon as I began praying, his eyelids began to flutter, then his hands started to shake. Resisting fiercely in his attempt to stay on his feet, he bent over backwards farther and farther until he looked like someone preparing to do the limbo. *He* was *not* under the influence of psychological suggestion!

A few weeks later I received a call to preach and share my testimony at a regional Vineyard pastors' retreat. Seventy Vineyard pastors and wives were there, every one pioneering new works in the Midwest and every one dead, dry, and burned-out. When I shared my testimony, God came and every person there except one got touched, and she was nailed before she got back home to Kentucky. I don't know how many times some of them got in line. My area overseer at the time, Steve Phillips, got in line six times. The sixth time we prayed for him he was knocked backwards into a bunch of chairs and instantly healed of a major spinal injury that had caused him much pain for five years.

A short time later Steve and the Regional Overseer, Happy Leman, attended the National Council of the Vineyard where Steve shared the testimony of his healing. One spiritually thirsty man there who was touched by that testimony was named John Arnott, pastor of a small church called the Toronto Airport Vineyard Christian Fellowship (now Toronto Airport Christian Fellowship or TACF). He was thirsty enough to risk asking me to come to his church.

When John invited me to Toronto he told me that he had heard about what had happened at the pastors' retreat. I told him that it might never happen again. That's how small my faith was. He insisted he still wanted me to come, even if nothing happened. He was willing to take that risk. I didn't want to fail alone, so he offered to pay the way for three or four others I would bring with me. Now, this was a thirsty man. Later on, when my son and others asked me what I thought would happen when I went to Canada, I told them that I just hoped God would show up. That's all I really wanted.

You see, I had a major problem that had hindered me throughout my ministry. It was something that four years of college, a seminary degree, all my training, and all my reading could not fix. My Achilles heel was that I believed that when "great" men of God such as John Wimber or Oral Roberts or Billy Graham said,

"Come, Holy Spirit," He would come, but if a nobody like Randy Clark said it, He might come, but probably not. I didn't know any better. I had no doubt at all of Christ's presence in my life. I knew that the Lord never leaves us or forsakes us and is always closer than a brother to us (see Heb. 13:5; Prov. 18:24). My problem was that I could not really believe that God would show up in manifested power when I prayed. I knew it in my head, but was unable to translate it into truth in my life.

This was because I projected onto God something of my earthly father. Now, my dad loves me. He always has and I have always known it. We had a good relationship when I was growing up except that I could not depend on him to be there for me. I grew up in poverty. Dad worked hard as a driller in the oilfields; he had to work long hours, sometimes double shifts. He had no choice. It was either work or be fired. He wasn't union. Many were the times I longed to see him in the stands when I was in a track meet or playing basketball or football, but he was not there. I knew it was because he was working, but it still hurt. Because I grew up unable to depend on my father to be there when I wanted him, I had always had a problem depending on God to be there too. My weakness was that I was afraid if I said, "Come, Holy Spirit," He wouldn't come.

The night before I left for Toronto, Richard Holcomb, a friend of mine in Texas, called with a word for me that he had received from the Lord. For over ten years God had used Richard supernaturally to speak into my life at times when I had a secret and desperate need for money or words of encouragement. That night he told me, "Randy, the Lord is saying 'Test Me now, test Me now, test Me now. Do not be afraid. I *will* back you up. I want your eyes to be open to see My resources for you in the heavenlies just as Elijah prayed that Gehazi's eyes would be opened. And do not become anxious, because when you become anxious you can't hear Me.'"

That prophetic word changed my life. I could not walk in my anointing without faith. Without faith it is impossible to please God (see Heb. 11:6). You could be the most anointed person in the world, but if you don't have faith to release that anointing, you will sit on it. That's where I had been. That very night before leaving for Toronto I went from saying, "I hope He comes," to "We are going to see more than we have ever seen— wonderful, powerful things that God is going to do." I wasn't just trying to convince myself; I was a positive man making a positive confession because of a prophetic word.

God showed up at Toronto and the renewal He began there is still going on and is spreading around the world. The glory is His alone. I can take no credit for what God has done. I couldn't heal myself. He changed me. From that day to this I have believed that every time I preach, God will touch people. I know it. I'm at the point now that until God shows me otherwise, people will be touched and healed at every meeting. God told me to test Him and He would back me up. I tested Him, and He has kept His word.

This is mercy. God set me up. He sovereignly chose a broken vessel, a pastor on the verge of a nervous breakdown and ready to quit, a pastor who was unable to believe that God would come when he prayed. Through it all God lovingly pursued me. He did something so unmistakably Him that it gave me the courage to come and drink. I simply responded to His pursuit. Since that day I have walked in a peace like nothing I have ever known before. In Tulsa, He completely healed my nervous condition. I never understood the Lord's words in Matthew 10:13 about pronouncing a blessing of peace until I experienced that peace. It truly is the peace that transcends all understanding (see Phil. 4:7).

Another thing He did in Tulsa was correct my angry spirit toward the faith camp people. He showed me how much they loved Him and He them, and I knew I needed to ask forgiveness for my heart attitude. This I did. There are still theological differences between me and the faith group, but I love them and enjoy ministering to them and with them.

Chapter 2

Mark Endres: The Bullfighters

When I invited Mark Endres to speak to the church one Sunday morning in July 1993, I really had no idea how prophetic he was. At the time Mark worked for a leading car manufacturer and, although not officially on staff, had pastored one of our home groups for a couple of years. He had done well, building his group over time to around 34. By his own admission, though, Mark had reached the point in January 1993 where he had lost his heart for ministry and for people. Their problems had become too much for him to bear. Like me, he was tired and burned-out.

Late in January 1993, Mark and several members of his home group met with me to discuss some of their problems and try to work them out. I remember that Mark didn't say much, but mainly listened. After talking for awhile I finally suggested that we pray. As Mark remembers:

> When they began to pray, something just broke in me. I hit my knees and said, "God, I know You're telling me the best fruit is at the end of the limb, but I don't want to climb out there. I know You're telling me the view is much better on top of the mountain, but I am too tired to climb. God, I want Your will, but I can't do this anymore." Then I just wept. I remember Randy behind me praying, "Lord, a humble and a contrite heart the Lord will not despise."
>
> Something happened to me then, but I had no idea where it was leading. The very next day, though, I realized that all of a sudden I wasn't tired of people anymore. God had restored my heart for ministry. I then remembered a note that a woman in the church had given me two weeks before where she described a vision in which she saw this happening for me. As a result of this, I began to come to the church sanctuary regularly after work or during lunch or on weekends just to pray by myself.

Over the next several months I began to notice Mark coming into the church regularly to pray, so one day I asked him what was going on. When he told me about having gotten his heart back, it prompted my invitation for him to speak to the church. I asked him to simply share what had been happening in his life.

Healing the Hurting

Mark's involvement with our church initially began because of a word of knowledge. He and his wife Tammy attended one of our home groups in 1991 during a time of great personal anguish and difficulty for them that no one else knew anything about. Mark was the victim of false accusations related to his running a state-funded program teaching mentally retarded adults to live independently in their own apartments. The mother of one of the women in the program had accused Mark of raping her daughter and withholding medication. The charges were blatantly false and Mark's employer knew it, but the woman was threatening legal action.

This had been going on for two weeks when Mark and Tammy attended their first home group meeting of the St. Louis Vineyard. They had told no one about their problems. Mark says:

> During one of the worship times a woman said, "I believe the Lord is saying that someone here is being falsely accused of something. The Lord wants you to know that He is aware of this and that He will take care of it for you." God came out of a doctrinal box for me that night. Tammy and I were really encouraged by this. That's how we became plugged into the church.

God followed through on His promise. Eventually, the accusations came to nothing and the crisis passed, but the whole thing was a major spiritual turning point for Mark and Tammy.

When Mark stood up to speak on that Sunday morning in July 1993, he had no idea of the condition I was in, how close I was to a nervous breakdown. He simply shared from his own experience and perspective as to what God had done in his life. Part of his message was a prophetic word about how God was going to bring hurting people into our church. Mark said that the only people who could comfort hurting or burned-out people were those who had experienced the same things themselves and had had the opportunity to walk with God through it.

It was around midnight that same Sunday that I received the "phone call from God" through my friend Jeff that set me on the road to Tulsa. After I went to Tulsa, got touched, and returned home, Mark's prophetic word was fulfilled as God began healing emotional needs and hurts in the church and started bringing in people with those kinds of problems.

Prophecy in Florida

In December 1994 another crisis arose in Mark's life involving false accusation as before, but this time regarding his employment with the car manufacturer. This was the catalyst for a sequence of events that God was orchestrating. A new supervisor accused Mark of conspiring with a subcontractor to steal a car from a dealership. There was no substance to the accusation, but the supervisor was known to the union as a "cut-throat," and in this case he wanted someone else in Mark's position and Mark had seniority. The union representative convinced Mark that if he stayed, the supervisor would find some way to get at him, and helped Mark obtain eight weeks of severance pay. With that, Mark resigned. It was just before Christmas. He tells what happened next:

On December 22, 1994, I was in my bedroom praying. "Lord, I don't understand it. I don't know why this is happening again. Is there something I have not learned?" There was no audible voice, but I felt God say to me, "Mark, this one you have to walk by faith, not by sight. How would it help you if I showed you the end result? You would still have to walk through it." I said, "God, maybe it would give me more hope. I don't have any right now." Then I felt Him telling me, "I'll peel back a corner and tell you this much. This will last one month and then it will be over."

My last day of work was December 28, 1994. During the week before I sent out 85 resumés. Randy was scheduled to conduct 15 days of meetings in Melbourne, Florida, beginning January 1, 1995. For the moment, there was nothing more I could do in the job search area, and because I felt a strong leading from God, I went with Randy to Melbourne for the first week of meetings. On the flight down I said to Randy, "I'm a young man. I've never seen a true move of God, and I want to."

During that week Randy and I roomed together and I helped out wherever I could in a general way just as a friend. At the end of the week we flew home for two days, then Randy would return for the second week. I wasn't planning to go back, but on the flight home Randy asked me, "You're thinking about coming back, aren't you?" I told him no, it wouldn't be fair to Tammy, and besides, I had to look for work. When I got home Tammy said, "You're going back, aren't you? I think the Lord told me you are going back for the second week."

I went back to Florida the next week, and about the fourth day we were there Randy was prophesied over by a couple known and respected by local pastors for their prophetic insight. Randy was told that God was going to give him an assistant to "carry your bag and pick up your glasses and help you remember things."

I was sitting in the first row and when I heard that, I felt overwhelmed and dropped to my knees, weeping. Several people from the church came and prayed over me. God did something right at that moment. Unknown to me, several people Randy knew and trusted had told him privately that they had seen me with him and that he needed me.

On January 28, 1995, Tammy and I went to dinner with Randy and his wife at their invitation. During dinner, Randy said, "Mark, I don't know where this ministry is going to go, but in faith we would like to take you on staff for three months with salary, and then see what happens. You commit three months to us and we will commit three months to you."

Tammy and I both felt fine about making the three-month commitment.

When we got home that evening I realized that it was a month to the day since I had left my job, just as God had told me. For me as well as for Tammy, this was pretty powerful confirmation.

Norwegian Word

Mark came on staff about the time my ministry began to intensify with a lot of invitations to do both domestic and international meetings. For two and a half years he traveled with me full-time, about 170 days a year. He participated in the meetings, helped minister, and managed the administrative details that came up on the road, such as fielding inquiries from pastors, doing paperwork, and taking care of information exchange. Very early on Mark began to display a profound prophetic gifting, receiving some of the most detailed and specific words of knowledge I have ever heard from anyone. One clear example of this was during our second trip to Trondheim, Norway, in April 1996.

It was the time of year in Norway when even at night it never gets any darker than dusk. We had gotten out of the meeting that night about 1:30 or 2:00 and still felt wide awake. We went over to the pastor's house along with some of his close friends and some church leaders. One couple there a prominent Norwegian evangelist and his wife, who were involved in missionary work in Russia. They ministered to poor

Russian churches, carrying them food supplies and other resources. We enjoyed a good time of fellowship, and then the people asked us to pray for them. It was about 3:00 a.m. when we started praying. Mark remembers:

I began to get very specific information for these people. As I prayed for them, I noticed that the others were either laughing or crying. I didn't know what was going on, but they said to me, "You can't imagine the accuracy of what you are praying over them." They were all very encouraged by it, and so was I. That night, God gave me a specific word for every person I prayed for—there were about a dozen of them—which had never happened before.

For example, concerning the couple doing missionary work in Russia, the Lord revealed to me the word that He would give them provisions for carrying to the poor churches in Russia. Also, He revealed to me that the evangelist's wife was deeply troubled emotionally. I knew nothing at all about either of these people before that night, but they verified the word regarding their ministry in Russia, and the wife was greatly encouraged simply by the knowledge that God knew where she was and what she was going through.

With another couple God revealed that the husband's Christian parents were starting to speak against some of the things he was trying to do. They were beginning a ministry to married couples and had been doing a lot of research. I told them that God was telling them to write some of their own material as well and put together a manual. They verified that all this was true, and they were greatly encouraged by this, knowing that God was in it, particularly since they had heard all this from someone who didn't even know them.

Guatemalan Nights

We ministered in Guatemala for the first time in November 1996. Those meetings were characterized by a lot of specific words of knowledge. Mark received a couple that were quite significant.

One night I shared a word the Lord had given me. "There is a young lady, a mother with three children. Just this week your husband committed adultery and has since left the house. As a result, you were out on the street this week begging for money for groceries." During the ministry time a young woman came to me and identified herself as the one I had spoken about. I prayed for her and she fell out in the Spirit. The two of her children who were there with her joined in laying hands on her.

The next night, the same woman came into the meeting accompanied by her husband. They came up to me later and the husband said, "I saw such a change in my wife that I had to come." I told him of his need to repent of his sin. He was ready. He said, "I am so sorry for what I have done to her in God's eyes. Will you pray for me? I need this broken in my life." As soon as I began praying, he broke into a profuse sweat, and then suddenly was flung back a couple of feet and to the ground, shaking. The shaking subsided in just a few minutes, but he was on the floor for a long time.

The third night, the two of them returned, their faces glowing. The man had brought two of his friends along and asked me to pray for them. Those two men came to know the Lord that night. Then we went back and ministered to the husband to break any soul ties he may have had with any of the women he had committed adultery with and to make sure everything was forgiven and reconciled between he and his wife. It was really incredible. God did an amazing work in their lives.

On another night, I received a rather unusual word. The Lord told me that there was someone at the meeting who had a family background involving bullfighting, which had created a lot of anger and dissension in the family and needed healing. Randy turned to me and said, "Mark, they don't have bullfighting in Guatemala." I told him, "I'm sorry, but if I missed it, I missed it." Later, a woman came to me and told me that her father and grandfather both were bullfighters and there was incredible anger and dissension between them. I prayed for her and she came back a couple of nights later to tell me that something had broken through at home and there had been repentance and a lot of love expressed between family members. I thought it was rather amazing that God would be interested in someone with a problem with bullfighting and anger, but that's what He was doing that night.

All in the Family

Late in 1996 we were in Philadelphia for a 30-day series of meetings. Again, Mark received some very specific words. One case is very interesting because he had words of knowledge for several members of one family, which also involved a significant healing.

The Lord showed me a mental picture of an African-American lady wearing blue slacks and a blue blazer, with a colorful scarf over her right shoulder. I said, "You have a condition in your hands that causes them to be dry and itch, and your daughter has recently been diagnosed with the same condition. You have a granddaughter who needs prayer also, but she has not been diagnosed with that condition." The woman came forward and was prayed for by another member of the ministry team. I met her the following day because she was the leader of a street evangelism team I was with. Her name was Pearl. She did have the condition I had spoken of and did have a daughter with the same problem.

The next night the word "Carmel" came to me. Then it changed to "Carmen," and finally, "Carmella." I said to Randy, "I think there is someone here named Carmella." As soon as I said that over the microphone, three ladies in the front row turned to their companion and said, "Carmella, that's you!" Carmella, a young African-American woman, came forward for prayer. I found out later that Carmel was a pet name that someone in her family called her, and that Carmen was a nickname used by other members of her immediate family. So God had shown me all three forms of her name. It was so funny. The funniest part, though, was that Carmella was Pearl's niece.

Carmella had another aunt who was there that night. She came up and introduced herself and said, "Earlier, when a word was given for tuberculosis, I didn't come up. I was too embarrassed." I said to her, "Let's pray now. I can't promise anything, but if you would like to receive prayer, we would sure love to do it." As we prayed for her healing, the Lord revealed that she was going to get some kind of opportunity at work. That encouraged her. I prayed for her that night. She went home to bed and woke up the next morning with a bad cough. She was pretty discouraged until all of a sudden she coughed up a lot of black stuff. She went to her doctor, who took chest X-rays that showed that her chest was completely clear. She brought the X-rays to the meeting that night.

It was amazing. God was all over that family. They were so encouraged. It was great to see God touch them that way.

A "Little Ole Me"

Mark Endres comes from a solid biblical and doctrinal background. He had a dramatic conversion to Christ during high school that resulted in an overnight change for him. From day one he received solid discipling, particularly through Campus Crusade for Christ, with whom he was involved while in college, and on whose staff he served for two years. According to Mark:

Because of the strong discipling I received, I developed a high regard for doctrinal correctness. Although there is nothing wrong with that—we need to be doctrinally sound—too strong a focus on doctrine can make it hard for us to relate to other Christians who may believe differently about some things than we do. If we are not careful, unity of the Body of Christ can be sacrificed for the sake of a doctrinal position. Where unbelievers are concerned, it is important that they come to know Jesus personally, rather than be converted to a particular doctrinal belief.

As I began to experience some things outside of my traditional frame of reference, I became more open with others who believed a little differently from me. Although these experiences did not define my doctrine, they definitely helped me re-analyze some of them. They brought God to a closer level with me. I began to learn to depend more on my walk with the Lord than on my own attempts to pursue Christian disciplines, particularly during difficult times. I also began to realize that not only was God sovereign over my life, but He was willing to let me know His thoughts.

That first visit to the home group was so encouraging when God revealed to others what only Tammy and I knew about. I told God later that I would love to be able to encourage others the same way. I believe that may have been the beginning of the prophetic gifting.

Not everyone comes into ministry with the same experience or background. The key to being used by God in ministry, whether it is healing, or prayer, or evangelism, or whatever, is not background and education and professional credentials nearly as much as it is availability and teachability. The important thing is to love people in Christ. Whenever we read about the activation of the spiritual gifts, they are presented in the context of doing all things in love. So if I have been trained to love the person first, then God can decide what gifts are going to be useful at that time.

Russian Reunion

Mark relates an incredible story from our first trip to Russia in 1996:

> When we were in Russia in 1996 for the first "Catch the Fire" conference, I received a surprise invitation to preach at a Moscow church on Sunday morning. I received a number of specific words for physical conditions, but we had to be out of the building by a certain time, so we met on the sidewalk for the ministry time. There were probably 600 people there, and we were praying publicly for these conditions. One woman in her late 30's or early 40's was brought to me with the assistance of two other people. She was unstable on her feet. Through a translator, I began to pray for her as she shared about some pain she was having in response to one of the words of knowledge. As I prayed for her, I sensed a prophetic word about her immune system. I said, "Lord, You know her immune system has broken down and is not operating properly. Lord, heal her immune system." She got very excited, telling the translator that that was one of her conditions. I said, "Lord, we thank You for revealing that. It means that You want to do something, so we pray that You will heal her immune system." Then I said, "Lord, I pray that what You do to her, You will do through her; that whenever she prays for sick people it will be the rule, not the exception, that they are healed." We left it at that.
>
> In May 1997 we returned to Russia for the second "Catch the Fire" conference. On the fourth night of meetings inside the huge sports complex, I saw a woman running across the

stage toward me during the ministry time. Her countenance was so bright she almost glowed in the dark. I didn't recognize her at first. She found a translator and identified herself. It was the same woman I had prayed for the year before. When I had first met her, she could not stand unassisted. Now she was running, leaping, and jumping. She looked so much younger, and very healthy. She said, "Mark, my immune system was completely healed after you prayed. Since then, I have been praying for the sick through my church. Just as you asked God, it is more often than not that people are healed when I pray for them." Then she said, "I was praying that you would be back so that I could thank you." Talk about a tear-fest! We have a wonderful God!

Chapter 3

Steve Phillips: Equipping the Body

If someone had said to me four years ago that I would visit 19 countries and speak to 175,000 people, I would have told him he was from the moon.

That's one way Steve Phillips describes how God has changed his life since the renewal began. Steve is not a newcomer to ministry, however. At the age of 18, he was an evangelist, and in the years since has been a youth pastor, an associate pastor, and a church planter. His service includes eight years as a senior pastor and four years as a counselor, administrator, and group therapist for a major Chicago area hospital. In addition, as part of the leadership team of Team Thrust for the

Nations, he helped train over 1,000 Christians in power evangelism ministry, and saw over 10,000 people come to the Lord in New York, New Orleans, Atlanta, Chicago, and other major cities. During this time he saw healings, miracles, and deliverances occur through the ministry of ordinary Christians.

Despite all this, Steve feels that none of it compares to what he has seen and experienced over the last four years. Speaking before a congregation in England, Steve commented on the current renewal and what he expects God to do in the days ahead:

> I've lived all my life for this moment. The last couple of years have had me more stirred than anything else in my life. It's like the last tick of the clock is going, and I'm ready for the explosion.

Divine Atomic Bomb

In the early 1970's Steve and his wife Jackie entered the Charismatic renewal, looking for a good balance between the activity of the Spirit and sound doctrinal and biblical teaching. They found it in the Vineyard association of churches. By 1993, Steve was the Vineyard Area Overseer for the Midwest with responsibility for 14 churches in three states, including mine in St. Louis. He was on the leadership team for the annual regional pastors' conference that year in Lake Geneva, Wisconsin, which I attended shortly after returning from Tulsa. Here is Steve's account of what happened:

Randy came to me during the conference and said that he had been touched by an unusual anointing and asked if he could share it with the meeting. The leadership team, of which I was a part, gave him a whole five minutes to share it in. Five hours later they were still picking us up off the floor. Randy simply told how God had touched him in Tulsa, and about the healings and conversions that resulted when he returned to his own church. The Spirit fell on that pastors' conference like an atomic bomb had hit. People were laid out all over the room, many of them Vineyard pastors going through rough times. For five hours they rested in the peace and love of God as the Spirit moved in them.

Steve himself was touched by God in a significant way. Five years earlier he had received a compression fracture of the fifth lumbar vertebra in his back after a refrigerator he was helping move slipped and fell against him. Ever since, he had suffered pain so bad that he usually was unable to sleep more than three hours a night. All of that changed during prayer time at the pastors' conference:

I came forward for prayer, and was the second one Randy prayed for. I fell out in the Spirit, but got up again after a few minutes. Randy came and prayed for me again. I fell out in the Spirit a second time. Every time I got up, Randy would come over and pray for me again, and each time, I fell out. This happened a total of six times. After the fifth time, I was beginning to get a little tired of it; after all, I was part of the leadership team responsible for coordinating things. Still, Randy prayed a sixth time and I went down a sixth time.

This time, though, I felt the pain in my back intensify, then subside. I got up a little later and thought no more about it.

The next morning there was no pain and I discovered that I had received at least an 80 percent healing. Jackie came into the room, saw me crying, and asked about the pain. I told her, "I think God healed me last night." Today, over four years later, even on my *worst* days I experience only about five percent of the pain I once had.

Appointment in Toronto

The next week Steve attended the National Council of the Vineyard in Anaheim, California, where he told of his healing and the five-hour soaking session at the pastors' conference. This led directly to John Arnott's invitation to me to come to Toronto. Steve was unaware of John's call to me, and four days after the National Council he flew to England, where he and Jackie were profoundly moved by the strong sense that God was preparing a mighty outpouring for that nation.

On the return flight to the United States, an interesting sequence of events began with an exchange between Steve and Jackie. As Steve describes it:

As we passed over Toronto, I turned to Jackie and said, "Before Whitney (our daughter) gets much older, we should take a train to Toronto so she can experience a train ride before it's too late. Who knows when the trains in America will be shut down?" Jackie looked at me as if I had had a stroke. "You *hate* the train!" I thought about that for a moment, then said, "You're right. I do hate the train. Why did I even say that? I don't even know if any trains go into Toronto."

A few days later I received a phone call from Randy. "Steve, you've *got* to come to Toronto! The same thing is happening here that happened at the pastors' conference. It's been going on for a week now, and I think it might even go a month!" I told Randy that there was no way I could come to Toronto; I had just returned home from three weeks overseas, I had no money, I couldn't be away from my church again so soon, and I had a lot of appointments set up. Randy asked me, "If all those things work out, will you come?" I asked him how soon he had to know. "Tomorrow," was his reply. I said, "Yes, Randy, if all those things work out by tomorrow, I'll be glad to come to Toronto." Before hanging up, Randy said, "John Arnott said to tell you that the Lord told him that this has something to do with an anointing touching the earth and a release of tools into the hands of God's people, and that you are supposed to be a part of it."

Now the Lord had given me that exact word about eight years before. I started to shake as I put the phone down. The next eight hours or so were incredible as I received one confirmation after another. A normally shy and quiet woman in my church came into my office and gave me a bold prophetic word about not having the faith to do what God wanted me to do— something completely out of character for her. Someone else called asking if I needed money. My appointments began canceling like crazy. I hit a snag when I called the travel agency and found I could not get a flight out in time. Driving home later, however, I passed a billboard that said, "Take the train." The travel agency confirmed that a train connection was available. Jackie and I were on our way to Toronto.

Steve was not impressed by the first service he attended at Toronto. A lot of things happened that he neither understood nor agreed with at first. When he arrived for the second night I asked him to share about his back being healed. He was scheduled to follow another speaker:

The man I was to follow got up to speak. He was *radiant*, like a 1,000-watt lightbulb. As he began to talk, I was shocked because his speech was almost unintelligible; it was slurred and strained and I had to listen very closely to understand anything. Basically, he was saying how happy he was in the Lord. I was even more amazed to learn that he was the pastor of a 1,300-member church and had a doctorate in theology. God had touched him a few days prior, and he had been unable to talk clearly since then. (He later regained his normal speech.) His joy was undeniable, though.

I felt God say to me, "Steve, you are so dry that you have forgotten what water tastes like. If I had to do that to you in order for you to have that kind of joy, would you be willing?" I began to weep uncontrollably. Even as they called my name and I rose to speak, the tears continued to flow. I could barely talk because of crying. I shared the best I could, then Randy told the group that the reason he had asked me to share was because he had received a word from the Lord about people with pain in the fifth vertebrae lumbar region of the back, and that if there were any who had that condition and wanted prayer, they should come forward and *I* would help Randy pray for them! I could barely talk, how could I pray?

Around 80 people came forward. As we began to pray they began to fall out in the Spirit. Carol Arnott came along praying, "Fill, Lord," with each one. I also ended up on the floor and became aware of a wonderful joy welling up inside me. I discovered that my speech had been affected in a way similar to the pastor's who had spoken before me. It was about nine weeks before all my speech faculties returned to normal. The joy of the Lord has remained.

Equipping the Body

Today, Steve's and Jackie's passion is to see the Body of Christ equipped to lead the lost to Jesus through the supernatural, prophetic witness of the Holy Spirit. Since their first trip to Toronto in January 1994, they have returned on more than 20 occasions to teach and minister. For over a year their focus was on ministering the renewal. In October 1995, they taught on evangelism for the first time, resulting in invitations from 104 pastors from around the world to come to their churches and teach.

In 1995, Steve resigned as the Midwest Area Overseer for the Association of Vineyard Churches, and traveled and taught full-time with Equipping Ministries International, a prophetic and evangelistic ministry that was based out of my church, the St. Louis Vineyard. At the present time, Steve conducts around

300 meetings a year. Of the 175,000 people he has spoken to in 19 countries since 1994, over 10,000 people have come to know the Lord.

Steve says that he is "incredibly surprised" that God has chosen to use him the way He has. He believes the key to being used by God is openness:

> I recall seeing Randy at Toronto, sitting during worship preparing his sermon because he simply had not had time to do it before, with all the conferences and meetings he had to attend. From this, I realized that God was using Randy because of his openness, not because of any personal dynamic or preparation, and that He could use me the same way.

Such is the impact of a "little ole me."

Chapter 4

Richard and Glenda Holcomb: A Watering Hole

My friendship with Richard and Glenda Holcomb dates back to January 1984, before I planted the Vineyard church in St. Louis. Through the years they have played a significant prophetic role in my life and ministry. Glenda remembers how we met:

> At that time we participated quite a bit with James Robison. On one occasion we took Richard's daughter LaJuana, who was in high school at the time and is deaf, to one of his conferences where John Wimber was teaching on healing. He taught that everybody could pray for the sick, and then had a clinic where everybody laid hands on people

and prayed for them. A lot of people prayed for LaJuana, including John Wimber, but Randy was the one who really stood out. He just kept praying and praying relentlessly, persevering. He wouldn't give up. A very special connection was made with him then. From time to time ever since God has connected us with very specific things to help Randy with and to be a support system and sounding board. It is a precious relationship that has grown through the years.

At different times God has spoken things to Richard regarding Randy, whether it was to send a certain amount of money or give a word of encouragement, or whatever, and every time it has happened, Randy has told us how significant it was at that particular time in his life. It is something that God has sovereignly done.

A former salesman for IBM, Richard entered the real estate business on the side in 1971, buying up and then reselling large tracts of land in the hill country of west Texas where he lives. The business prospered, and in 1978 he quit IBM to go full-time. Richard gives God all the credit for his success. Even during the mid-1980's, when many land developers in Texas went bankrupt, Richard's business continued to do well. He relates one example:

God sovereignly spoke to me about one transaction. In 1985 or 1986, as I was preparing to make one of the biggest deals I had ever made, I felt God say to me, "Don't do it. If you do, you're going to pay for it." I backed off of that one. As it turned out, the man who eventually bought that deal went bankrupt, as did many others, including some who were quite wealthy. God saved my business in the mid-80's. We are not wealthy, but God has given us independence.

That independence has made it possible for Richard to participate in many mission trips and conferences. For example, in 1997 Richard was with me in Argentina when I held some meetings jointly with Cindy Jacobs. She had an affirming prophetic word for Richard:

> Halfway through one meeting she stopped, looked at me, and said, "I see that you are a businessman and that you understand commodities and buying and selling. You are to stay in business, but you also will be going out on your own more in 1998, speaking. But God doesn't want you out of business. He wants you to do both." That was a strong confirmation to me of what God told me two or three years ago, that I was a businessman, but was also to go pray for people. That's what I feel comfortable doing on these mission trips: praying for people.

Toronto Prophecy

As I mentioned in Chapter 1, Richard called me the night before I left for Toronto in January 1994 with a prophetic word for me that changed my life. According to Richard:

> I was driving around Kerrville, Texas, one day doing my work when I felt God say to me, "Call Randy." At first I let it pass; it was the kind of impression you get from time to time to call a friend to see how he is doing. The next morning God spoke to me again: "Call Randy." As I was returning home at

the end of the day, for the third time I got a strong impression to call Randy.

The first time I called, Randy wasn't home. When I told his wife, DeAnne, why I had called she insisted that I needed to speak directly to Randy and asked me to call back. Glenda told me I should write down my impressions, so I scribbled them on a piece of paper. When I spoke to Randy early that evening, I was marching around my living room with my portable phone, like a general telling the troops to take off and get after it.

I said, "Randy, I got a strong impression that God is looking for someone who will push to the 'nth' degree and never give up; who will move forward and not look back." Randy asked if I had received any Scripture with it. I said, "Yes, 'Test Me now' (see Mal. 3:10b). God wants your eyes open even as Gehazi's eyes were opened to see the chariots of fire (see 2 Kings 6:8-17). God wants you to see the resources He has for you. Whatever you speak, God will back you up. Period. You speak it, God will confirm it."

I am an emotional and dramatic person by nature, and I came on pretty strong to Randy that night. After I hung up, Glenda challenged me about it. She asked, "Do you *know* that word was from God? If it wasn't, you may push Randy over the edge." I had to admit that I didn't know for sure. A couple of days later, on Saturday night, I was praying around midnight, asking God to show me if I had done the right thing with Randy. I wanted confirmation. I don't mind telling people things, but I need to know if what I say is right or wrong.

Then, as clearly as I have ever heard anything, God said, "I want you to write this down and send it to Randy before you hear anything back from him. I am elevating Randy to a new level of recognition all over the world. There is good, better, and best. You are in the 'best.' It is like a professional golfer who breaks through and wins a major tournament." The Lord also gave a warning. "Randy needs three people to back him up, who will pray without ceasing for him; people who are very strong in their own right and won't draw from him, but give to him, support him, and undergird him. They are like the mighty men of David (see 2 Sam. 23) who have accomplished things already. Behind those, he needs 30 more who are almost at that level, but not quite, because Randy needs that prayer covering in partnership with him."

Double Anointing

After the renewal broke out in Toronto, I called Richard and asked him to come to Toronto. Everything had begun to happen just as Richard had said in the word he received from the Lord. It took a little persuading, but he finally agreed to come. It was in the latter part of February 1994 when he arrived. While there, Richard received another prophetic word. This one was extremely powerful and dramatic, an Old Testament-style prophecy where God sovereignly took over his body and expressed the word in speech and action. This is how Richard describes it:

One day we were through and getting ready to go to lunch and Randy said, "I'm exhausted." I said, "I don't blame you." We were staying up till 2:00 or 3:00 in the morning; anybody would be tired. Randy asked me to pray for him to be refreshed. I said, "God, refresh him now." The power of God hit him and he hit the floor. Then all of a sudden the power of God came upon my body and it was just awesome. Earlier, I had heard some people say everything going on at Toronto was about to stop, that it was a dead horse. Now, fury rose up within me. I said, "No! This is not a dead horse. What we are seeing now is the engine, not the caboose; and the fuel that will fire this engine is the Holy Spirit." With that, my arms started going like helicopters in giant circles and I couldn't control them. Then God said to me, "These are circles with double anointing and double power." I got the impression that God was emphasizing that He was doubling it and it wasn't going to be something normal, but something supernatural—great power and great anointing.

The next thing I knew, I began speaking in another language, like an Indian dialect. I had never done that before and it felt so strange. God said, "Randy is going to go to nations that don't speak the English language." Suddenly, it seemed that all the energy drained out of my body, and I hit the floor. I couldn't stand up anymore. I said, "God, I can't move." He sent me a strong rebuke right then and there. He said, "No, you don't decide when you stop. Get up from there right now and tell Randy the same thing. He may get tired, but he will never decide when he is going to quit. This is like Moses when his arms got tired. I will send people to hold his arms up when he gets tired. The potter will tell the clay what he is to do; the clay will never tell the potter what he is to do."

After this, I cried real hard, not about the Holy Spirit, but because I saw all this leading Randy not to a pedestal, but to the cross. I knew he would suffer for what God was going to do through him.

West Texas Watering Hole

Before the renewal began, Richard and Glenda were working in a small church in Ingram, Texas, that had begun from a jail ministry and from reaching people off the street. They developed and led Christian 12-step programs to help the church grow. After they became involved in the renewal, they began to have some of the renewal leaders visit in their home and minister in their church. I have been there, as well as Larry Randolph, Graham Cooke, and several others.

Early in the summer of 1997, Richard and Glenda and a number of others moved out from their church into a new venture of faith. They rented a conference room at a small hotel and began holding meetings. Several months later they established a non-profit organization called Impact Ministries, which is reaching out into the community to foster unity among the many and different churches in the area. They have sensed that God wants them to be a "watering hole" for the work of the Spirit in the hill country of west Texas, where renewal has not really taken hold yet.

The ministry that Richard and Glenda are now involved in is not a church in the traditional sense. According to Richard:

God spoke to us that we were to go outside the four walls and not to have a normal church. There won't be a model for what we will be doing. Instead, we will create the model. So, we are really seeking God's breath behind what we are doing. God is putting it together. I think it is going to be totally different, not just from the standpoint of helping people and praying for people, but from the standpoint of governmental structure and a focus on house meetings as opposed to putting money into a building.

God has shown us that what we have seen so far is really nothing, and that what lies ahead has the potential to rock the whole earth.

Glenda adds:

We feel that we are going to be an equipping center. I believe God has spoken that we are going to be a watering hole down here, and have the ability to unite pastors and churches in our area that nobody has ever been able to do before. We are already seeing some of that. It may be a slow process, but we are going to connect with these people, bring some unity that has never existed, and light the fires of the Holy Spirit in this area. We feel a call to evangelize the hill country, and we are trying to learn how God wants it done.

Concerning the impact of the renewal, Richard says:

All of us, the common people in the churches, are being encouraged with the truth that God will impart His Spirit and His power to us and that He wants to work through us. We are being given the confidence and faith that God will use us even if we are not pastors or other leaders in the church.

God wants to use us and will use us very mightily if we allow Him to. This is one of the most important impacts of Randy's ministry. Common people are rising up to say, "I can!" This is a nameless, faceless revival, and it is the people in the pews who are doing it. That's Randy's legacy.

Glenda adds:

Randy's ministry is activating the "little ole me's." John Wimber used to teach on healing, then say, "Let's do the stuff," and follow with the clinic where everybody would pray for each other. I think that mantle was passed from John Wimber to Randy because Randy is really getting all the "little ole me's" to "do the stuff."

Another thing is that Randy is not just trying to get the "little ole me's" to pray for healing; he's also getting the ordinary people to send and be sent to go to the nations. That has been a big focus of what Randy is called to do. We are all becoming more globally aware and are beginning to move out of our own areas where many of us have been all our lives.

Personally, the renewal has affected Richard and Glenda deeply. Glenda says:

We are just really blessed to be a part of it. God has brought it about and we just feel so honored and humbled to be involved in what God is doing right now and to be able to invest in this move of the Spirit with our lives and our finances and whatever else we have.

Richard adds:

The most exciting thing I have ever done is what I'm doing right now. It gives me my life. It gives me my energies and my thought patterns. This is what gives meaning and purpose to me. My job is a vehicle that provides the money, but this is what really motivates me. It is what trips my trigger, so to speak. I absolutely love it, and I thank God for allowing me the opportunity to be involved in it.

Chapter 5

Steve Long: The Holy Spirit's Agenda

Steve Long says that it is scary sometimes to walk in the things of the Spirit:

> I've spoken in churches where I have made such a key difference, because of what the Holy Spirit has done in one evening, that the church's entire philosophy of how to think, act, and operate has changed. I'm very thankful for the opportunity God has given me to help shape churches, but at the same time I must be very careful that I am speaking on behalf of the Holy Spirit and not letting the flesh, Steve Long, get in the way.

In September 1997 I visited a church in Glasgow, Scotland. I had been there once before. One Sunday night we had a healing service, and about 100 people came forward for prayer. Of the 75 I personally prayed for, all except two were healed. That's what it is like when the Spirit is there and in control. If the flesh is in charge, the meeting will probably be a disaster.

Steve Long is one of the "old-timers" of the renewal, having been involved almost from the very beginning. An associate pastor for a Baptist church in Mississauga, near Toronto, in January 1994 Steve was "loaned" to John Arnott's church, the Toronto Airport Christian Fellowship, after the second week of renewal. He was to help organize and administrate the remaining meetings, which at that time we all expected to continue for only a couple more weeks.

Six months later, with renewal still going strong, Steve formally joined the staff at the Toronto Airport Christian Fellowship. For three and a half years he coordinated the evening renewal meetings at the church. Since September 1997 Steve has served as one of three area pastors for the Toronto church, which sits almost on the border of three cities: Toronto, Mississauga, and Brampton. Steve has pastoral responsibility for the city of Toronto itself. He also coordinates the various conferences hosted by the church.

From the beginning Steve's Baptist church and the Toronto Airport church have enjoyed a good relationship.

Steve and his senior pastor, John Freel, had known John Arnott for a couple of years prior to renewal through attending some of the pastors' days that John Arnott had sponsored. About the relationship, Steve says:

> We felt very comfortable coming here, so there wasn't really any competition. In fact, we were very happy at our Baptist church to have the renewal meetings going because we could send our people over for refreshing and to get their lives in order and all that kind of thing. It was a good relationship from a leader's standpoint.

Touched in Toronto

Originally, I was invited by John Arnott to do a weekend series of meetings, Thursday through Sunday, January 20-23, 1994, and I planned to return to St. Louis after the Sunday service. That all changed when "God showed up" at the first meeting. Before the weekend was over, John asked me to stay over a couple of days so there could be a Monday night meeting. I agreed, and that Monday John burned up the phone lines calling pastors and others he knew in the area and encouraging them to come. Steve Long was one of those. He shares what happened:

> John called me on Monday afternoon and told me about the meetings they had had over the weekend. He told me about some people getting healed and others being set free from addictions. Many people had experienced wonderful breakthroughs in their lives. John also described the effect of the Holy Spirit: people shaking, laughing, and being drunk in

the Spirit. I also spoke for about 20 minutes to Randy Clark, whom I had never met or even heard of until then. Then John came back on the phone and encouraged me to do whatever I needed to do to be at the meeting that night.

I called John Freel, my senior pastor and good friend, and my brother Richard, who pastored another Baptist church, and that night the three of us and our wives went to the meeting. Like all good Baptists, we sat in the back row. John Arnott introduced us to Randy. It was a real quick thing, 30 seconds or so, just before the meeting began. All six of us were profoundly touched that night.

Randy gave a message and then invited people to come forward who needed to be saved, or who needed to recommit their lives to Jesus, or who needed refreshing in their spiritual lives—those who loved and served the Lord but who were feeling drained and tired and ready to give up. All six of us should have responded to that one, but John Freel's wife, Anne, was the only one of our little group who went forward. Randy prayed with her and she began to weep. It was very interesting for us, standing in the back watching the ministry time, because people were laughing and falling and all this kind of thing, and we were all thinking, *This is bizarre*, and yet we knew Anne. Eventually, Anne composed herself and came back to our row. Suddenly, she started to giggle and then just laughed at us. She fell over on her chair. It was so strange for us to see Anne Freel like that. We knew something was happening.

After the ministry team finished praying for everybody who had come forward, they started praying for everyone who *hadn't* come forward; something pretty dangerous, in my opinion. Randy didn't start with the people up front, though. He came straight to us. He asked who he could pray for, and we all pointed to each other jokingly, none of us wanting to be the first. Anne was laughing at all this. Randy waved his hand at her as if to say, "More, Holy Spirit," and she fell over again. It was amazing to me that with just a wave of the hand a person would fall. My brother Richard and his wife received prayer, and both of them fell to the floor. This shocked me; after all, *this was my brother*! That really got my attention. Randy prayed for John Freel then, and John began to shake, not violently but enough that I could see something was going on. John and I had pastored together for five years and been friends for another four or five before that, and I had never seen him like this.

Then Randy asked, "Can I pray for you and Sandra?" We didn't know what to expect, but closed our eyes and put our hands out in front of us as we had seen everyone else doing. As soon as Randy began praying, my wife and I both felt very weak in the knees. We had never had an encounter with God like this, where we experienced His Presence that immediately and that strongly. For some dumb reason I did not want to fall backwards. It was as if to fall backwards would mean the end of life as I knew it. I didn't know what I would be getting into, so I just slumped straight down onto my knees and collapsed. It was quite uncomfortable.

I did what John and Randy had asked everyone to do: I lay there waiting for and listening to the Holy Spirit. I was aware of everything that was going on around me, but I was also aware of an incredible peace and freedom from anxiety. I didn't realize then that it was the peace of God; I just knew that it was very relaxing.

Driving home a little later, Sandra and I discussed the meeting. We both had problems in our minds putting together everything we had seen and experienced, yet we both felt in our spirits that it was genuine and that God had been present in great power at the meeting. We had never seen anything like it. It was certainly quite different from the services in our Baptist church.

The following Thursday, John Freel and I had lunch with John Arnott and Randy Clark (obviously, Randy had not gone home after the Monday meeting—the renewal was too strong!), just to ask some questions about what was happening. John Arnott and Randy were not very helpful. Every time we asked, "What does this mean?" they would say, "We have no idea." All of this was brand-new to them too, but because Randy and John Arnott both had Baptist backgrounds, they knew where we were coming from. John Freel and I both were charismatic in theology, but not in practice. Our non-charismatic Baptist church was very open to receiving more from the Spirit, though, so we were ready to be touched.

Changes of the Heart

Steve noticed some immediate changes in his attitude and perspective, both in his spiritual life and his family relationships. By his own admission, even though he was a pastor, he had been "going through the motions" as a Christian, and was "just hopeless" in the personal disciplines of prayer and Bible study. After God touched him that Monday night in Toronto, things began to change. According to Steve:

The next morning I woke early, around 5:00, completely refreshed and ready to go, and with such a desire to pray and study the Bible again. I read through the entire Book of Acts and began researching every passage that talked about the Holy Spirit. I wanted to re-study for myself what the Holy Spirit was all about rather than just taking the information from books. The Book of Acts and the Epistles began to come alive for me. I became convinced that everything I had seen the night before was legitimate and within the Scriptures.

During the first month the Lord began healing major character flaws in my life without anyone ever praying for me for those areas. For one thing, I had always been very critical toward my wife, and for another, I was very impatient toward my two boys. One afternoon after work I came home and Sandra asked if we could talk. That was usually the prelude to something unpleasant, so I didn't know what to expect. Sandra said, "Do you realize you have changed? In the last month you haven't yelled at me or the boys once, and you haven't been critical about things the way you once were." I began to cry because these were problems I was well aware of but had never been able to deal with successfully. I realized that God had sneaked up on me and in His love entered the back door of my heart and begun to heal those areas.

The Spirit's Agenda

Steve has also experienced a dramatic change in his attitude and approach toward ministry. He is very detail-oriented and a gifted administrator who has always enjoyed and thrived on tackling the logistics end of planning conferences, seminars, and such. The Holy Spirit made some adjustments in these areas as well.

One of the first things God asked me to do was to stop using my planning skills and instead to be dependent on Him. He asked me to throw away my checklist for conference planning. I deleted it from my computer, got rid of all my planning sheets, and just began to listen to Him and allow the Holy Spirit to help me plan things. I have really enjoyed the change. It was a challenge at first, because I was always afraid that I would forget something, but I discovered that not only was I still able to plan, but the Holy Spirit also gave me insights into things that were going to come up that I couldn't have planned for otherwise. I would dream at night about the conference and would talk through the scenarios of what might happen in a particular situation and what to do about it. It was like a question and answer session with God. The next morning I would know just what to do and would make changes accordingly. It was a big change for me to learn to recognize and follow the promptings of the Holy Spirit in that way.

Another big change came in my preaching. Once, I was very much bound to notes and to writing out a full manuscript before I preached. That's how I was trained: lots of research and a three-point sermon. Early on in the renewal I felt the Lord ask me to listen to Him more, as opposed to pre-planning it myself. Many times the Holy Spirit has asked me to wait on Him concerning what I should preach. There have even been a few times when I was introduced and was standing up to speak and still didn't know what I was going to say. On those occasions the Holy Spirit has given me thoughts from some previous research or from an earlier devotional time, and I have found an incredible liberty in the Spirit to speak on the things He has brought to mind.

Most of my adult life I have had a desire for people to notice me, pat me on the back, and tell me how good I am. Even though I didn't realize it for a long time, I was always looking for attention and trying to impress my colleagues, denominational leaders, and even people in my church. Once God began to heal me of this and I started to learn to get my significance from God rather than other people, my entire philosophy of ministry changed dramatically.

I have found it extremely interesting that as I have learned to worry less and less about getting attention, God has started giving me more attention than I would ever have dreamed of before, simply due to the fact that I am on the staff of a church that receives international attention. I have come to realize that it isn't me, but the gifting God has given me. As I have sought to humble myself more and more and give the Lord more and more attention, it seems that almost the opposite happens, and He uses me more and more.

When Randy says, "God can use little ole me," I identify completely because I was at a place of extreme frustration with where my life was going, and struggling with my character flaws. It was a complete surprise to discover that God would use me to preach and see people's lives changed for Christ; to see people healed physically, emotionally, and spiritually. It's absolutely wonderful to know that God can use dysfunctional people like me.

Steve has some further insights regarding the qualities of a "little ole me":

Humility is very important, particularly in the sense of recognizing that it is God who does the work, not us. The more we get ourselves out of the way, the more room God has to demonstrate His power and glory. "Little ole me's" are people who know that if God is not with them, they are nothing. Randy is very much like that. He knows that if the Holy Spirit doesn't show up in his meetings, they will be a disaster. The same is true with me. There has to be a real dependence on God.

Chapter 6

Fred Grewe: Freedom and Deliverance

"Contrary to what many say, I don't believe there's a problem of too little evangelism in North America. Instead, we have a freedom problem. If we were really free, non-Christians would be ripping the doors off our churches to find out what we've got. The problem for the most part is, they don't want to be like us. We claim to be redeemed, yet we can act just as, or more neurotic and uptight, than many of them do."[1]

Fred Grewe has a heart for freedom and deliverance; he wants to see people set free from sin and delivered from spiritual, emotional, and psychological bondage caused by sin as well as from demonic influence. One reason for this is personal experience. Fred knows what it is like to be in spiritual bondage; he also knows what it is like to be sovereignly set free. This former Roman Catholic now travels as an itinerant renewal preacher with an international schedule. He also participates frequently on my ministry team and often trains teams to assist with inner healing and deliverance ministry. He is truly a "little ole me" that God has raised up. Fred says:

> "Three years ago, when I pastored a small church in Melbourne, Florida, I couldn't get 100 people to listen to me preach if I handed out $100 bills. But then God's Spirit hit us. We experienced eight-and-a-half incredible months of nightly renewal meetings in 1995. During that time God led me to resign my post as a pastor and join the itinerant speakers' circuit."[2]

Raised Roman Catholic, Fred found Christ in 1971 in a Franciscan friary when a Catholic priest using the tract *The Four Spiritual Laws* led him to the Lord. For the next nine years he was actively involved in the Charismatic movement in the Roman Catholic Church. In 1980 God led him into the Vineyard churches, where he pastored and helped to launch four churches before entering his present itinerant ministry.

Because of his Catholic background, Fred has a deep appreciation for the importance of some aspects of the Christian life that are neglected by much of the Protestant Church. One example is confession of sin. "As Protestants," Fred says, "we have 'thrown the baby out with the bathwater' when it comes to confession." The Christian Church in North America has failed to face up to the seriousness of sin and does not adequately recognize the problem of spiritual bondage, particularly among the people in the churches, much less the lost outside. This awareness has led to his belief that the problem in North America is not a lack of evangelism, but a lack of freedom, and fuels the fire of his desire to minister freedom and deliverance to people.

Words of Knowledge

By his own description, Fred has always been a "hard-to-receive" person. Even as a Vineyard pastor he would pray for people and they would be hit by the Spirit, but nothing would happen to him. He describes the night when all that changed:

> When I first got into the renewal, in Wilmington, North Carolina, Randy prayed for me one night, and I got blasted. I turned into Benny Hinn that night. I was praying for everybody; they were shaking and falling. I was the man of the hour. It was incredible. It seemed like everyone I prayed for was hit by the Spirit; everyone, that is, except for the last man I prayed for. Nothing happened to him. I was kind of bummed. What happened? Where did it go?

> The man had been videotaping the meeting, and since I had some knowledge and experience with video, I started talking to him. I asked him what he was doing with his life. He said that he wasn't really in video, but just did it on the

side. He felt that God had told him to move to another city, but he was involved with a girl and was reluctant to go. Just then God spoke to me. I asked the man if he knew what the word *prodigal* meant. He stumbled around a little, then I said, "The word *prodigal* means 'to waste.' The great sin of the prodigal son was that he wasted his inheritance. The Lord has told me that you are wasting His inheritance. He has told you to move and you have disobeyed Him."

As soon as I said this, he let out a yell and fell back on the floor. He lay there, moaning, and I was saying, "God, get him. Holy Ghost, get him." Several people were standing around watching this. I let it go on for five or ten minutes. I would come back every few minutes and say, "God, get him some more," because I wanted the Lord to burn that disobedience out of him. Then I came over and prayed for the peace of God to come on him and release him.

In May 1997 Fred took part in a "Praying Down the Fire" conference I hosted in St. Louis. A pastors' meeting preceded the conference proper. It was a couple of hours for questions and answers about the renewal and where things were headed. At the end of the discussion we had a ministry time. There was no music; there had been no worship time. I asked Fred to help me. As he came forward, he told me that he had a word of knowledge and I asked him to share it. Fred remembers:

I said, "The Lord has told me that there are some men here who are addicted to pornography and masturbation. I will be in the back corner. If that is you, come on back and I'll pray for you." This was at a pastors' meeting! Fifteen or 16 people came back for prayer.

One man I prayed for raises money for a Christian college in Kentucky, and he told me later that he had been addicted to masturbation since he was 12. When he came for prayer, I didn't know who he was. I had never met him, but the Lord gave me a word of knowledge for him. The Lord said, "This man is a perfectionist. His standards are so high that when he doesn't meet them he retreats into a fantasy world for comfort." As soon as I said that, he was knocked over by the Lord and was liberated at that instant. He has been free ever since. He has even written about his experience and has shared it in many churches. There is power in freedom and deliverance.

Deliverance in Philadelphia

Fred has a tremendous story of deliverance that took place in Philadelphia during a deliverance ministry training conducted by the Argentinian pastors and leaders who have worked in deliverance for years. At that time, Fred was himself just learning the model and the process for ministering deliverance. During a break in one of the sessions, Fred was talking with the wife of a pastor who had helped to coordinate and oversee the entire Philadelphia meeting. As Fred recalls:

Janet had suffered terrible migraine headaches for years, and now she had another one. She was getting ready to go home because she simply couldn't take the pain. I said, "This is ridiculous. Here we are at a meeting to learn how to get free of things, and you're being attacked." In the good old Vineyard way I had learned, I prayed for healing, and nothing happened. Then I thought, *Oh Lord, I bet this is a demon.* I had never felt comfortable dealing with demons or demonic deliverance, but I thought I needed to try. After all, I was attending a conference to learn how to break the power of oppressive spirits. So, I prayed again. "Lord, break the power of this evil spirit. Janet is a good Christian woman; this thing has no right to her." I said to the spirit, "I break your power in the name of Jesus." I tried with vim and vigor, just as I had always been taught. When I said, "You have no right to her," a voice inside my head said, "Yes, I do." I ignored the voice and prayed again. Nothing happened. Her head was still throbbing.

I told Janet I was sorry, and she got her coat and was ready to walk away. Then she turned and said, "By the way, when you prayed, 'You have no right to her,' I heard a voice in my head say, 'Yes, I do.'" I said, "I heard the same thing. Let's pray again." I felt more certain now that a demon had shown himself, so, as we were learning at the conference, I began interviewing Janet to find the root cause of the problem. She told me she had suffered migraines for 14 years, so I asked her what had happened 14 years before.

She told me that her mother-in-law and father-in-law had come to visit them before going to Israel on a trip, and that during the visit her mother-in-law got sick and started having terrible headaches. The trip to Israel was cancelled and Janet's mother-in-law spent the next year and a half in and out of the hospital and she and her husband lived for awhile with Janet and her family. At the same time, Janet was pregnant with their second child, who was born after a difficult labor. Shortly after the birth, Janet's husband was called away on work much of the time, and Janet was left at home to care for her in-laws and her newborn baby. It had been a terrible time, and it was then that Janet's migraine headaches had begun.

At this point, God gave me a word of knowledge for her. He told me that Janet was afraid that what had happened to her mother-in-law was going to happen to her, and that she felt also that God had deserted her during this time. I thanked the Lord for these words and began to pray. I said, "Lord, I just pray that You will relieve Janet of this fear that what happened to her mother-in-law will happen to her." As soon as I said this, Janet started jerking and crying, and I knew I had hit something. I continued praying, "Lord, will You forgive her that she felt like You deserted her?" Now Janet was really crying. After that, I knew we had it, so I said, "Now, spirit, in the name of Jesus, I break your power over this woman." Instantly, her migraine stopped.

A month later, when I returned for the start of the meetings, Janet told me that for the first time in 14 years she was off her pain medication. She didn't need it anymore. Once the power of the oppressive spirit was broken, Janet had been instantly and completely delivered.

Fred believes that Janet's problem is not uncommon, but widespread, even in North America. What complicates it is that we are too sophisticated to recognize it. According to Fred:

> "We have just as many devils here as anywhere else. We just give them fancy names like compulsions, phobias, neuroses, addictions. We Christians must deal lovingly with people who are tormented by these things. It is our mandate. It is for freedom that Christ has set us free (see Gal. 5:1). Our responsibility, as Christians, is to experience freedom, and to give it away, not just theologize about it."[3]

Endnotes

1. Fred Grewe, "There Are Devils in Your Church," *Spread the Fire* (August, 1997), 14.

2. Grewe, "Devils in Your Church," 14.

3. Grewe, "Devils in Your Church," 15.

Chapter 7

The Biblical Basis for Healing

One night I was preaching in Guatemala City on the biblical basis for healing. About five minutes into the sermon, a woman in her 40's stood up off to my right. I looked at her and said in Spanish, "God bless you." She went down on the floor and was out for the rest of the sermon. After I finished preaching we had a time of impartation. Many people came forward, including a ten-year-old boy named Daniel. I prayed for him and he hit the floor, shaking violently and crying. You could just feel the compassion of God for healing. The middle-aged woman couldn't see this, though, because she was still on the floor from earlier. However, when she got up a little later, God told her to go to Daniel and have him pray for her. She did, and then God sent her to the pastor's wife to receive prayer.

This woman returned the next night with her medical records in hand and a remarkable testimony. The day before, she had been scheduled for a hysterectomy and had postponed it to come to the meeting. Her uterus was full of tumors. After receiving prayer, she visited her doctor and insisted on another examination before surgery. The doctor told her that she didn't need one because he had examined her two days before. She insisted, saying, "I believe Jesus healed me." The doctor was a skeptic; he didn't believe in divine healing. Nevertheless, he examined her again. He then wrote on her chart that not only were no tumors found, but her uterus was like that of a 20-year-old woman.

Miraculous healings such as this one are happening all over the world during this wonderful period of God's visitation and renewal. This story illustrates two important things about healing: God heals miraculously, and He often uses ordinary people to do it. The Guatemalan woman was prayed for by a ten-year-old boy and a pastor's wife, and God completely healed her.

Many Christians today wonder whether or not God still heals. Many churches teach that healing was for the first century Church, not for today. As a result, many believers have little or no expectation for God to do anything in the area of healing. But what does the Word of

God say? Are there biblical grounds for the belief that God still heals today?

The God Who Heals

The first thing we need to understand is that God has revealed Himself in the Bible as a God who heals. In Exodus 15:26, God is speaking to His covenant people, the Israelites, promising that if they will listen to and obey Him, He will not bring on them any of the diseases with which He afflicted the Egyptians. The very last part of the verse says, "...for I am the Lord, who heals you." That is the foundation. The God of the Bible is a God who heals.

The Gospels reveal that healing was a prophetic indication of who the Messiah would be and of how He would be recognized. At the height of his popularity, John the Baptist had boldly proclaimed that his cousin, Jesus of Nazareth, was the Messiah, the Lamb of God who was to take away the sin of the world. Later, in the darkness of Herod's dungeon, he wasn't so sure. It is easy to have faith when you are popular and everyone is coming to you, but much harder when you have been isolated and spoken ill of. John needed reassurance, so he sent two of his disciples to ask Jesus directly. Luke recorded the exchange: "When the men came to Jesus, they said, 'John the Baptist sent us to You to ask, "Are You the one who was to come, or should we expect someone else?" ' " (Lk. 7:20) Jesus replied:

..."Go back and report to John what you have seen
and heard: The blind receive sight, the lame walk,
those who have leprosy are cured, the deaf hear, the
dead are raised, and the good news is preached to the
poor. Blessed is the man who does not fall away on
account of Me"* (Luke 7:22-23).

These verses reflect Isaiah 61:1-2, the same passage
Jesus read in the synagogue in Nazareth one Sabbath
(see Lk. 4:16-21), when He followed the reading with
the words, "Today this scripture is fulfilled in your
hearing" (Lk. 4:21). The Messiah would be a healer
who fulfilled not only Isaiah 61:1-2, but also, as the
Suffering Servant, Isaiah 53: "...and by His wounds we
are healed" (Is. 53:5b).

As healing was a sign of the Messiah, so it is also a
sign of His Church—His people, those who have been
called out to follow Him. Healing was also a sign of the
anointing of God. Luke 4:18-19 says:

*The Spirit of the Lord is on Me, because He has
anointed Me to preach good news to the poor. He has
sent Me to proclaim freedom for the prisoners and
recovery of sight for the blind, to release the
oppressed, to proclaim the year of the Lord's favor*
(Luke 4:18-19).

Both the Hebrew word *mashiyach* (Messiah) and the
Greek word *christos* (Christ) mean "the anointed one."
Jesus was the Anointed One. As His followers, we are
anointed ones also. A sign of the anointing is healing.
What I am getting at is that *healing is part and parcel*

of the gospel; it is not peripheral to it. It is not a side issue. People say we need to keep "the main and the plain things." I'm saying that healing is clearly part of the "main and plain things," although it is not considered to be so by many parts of the Church today.

We, as the Body of Christ, His expression on earth today, should still have the anointing of God on us. We represent Him. As His ambassadors, we carry His authority, so we should see some of the things take place today as happened in Jesus' day.

In the summer of 1997 while in Argentina, an elderly woman came up to us. She had been blind for three years and had a severe colon problem. We prayed for about an hour and God healed her colon. We then prayed for her eyes for another hour. Gradually, she began to get her sight back. First, she said she could see shadows. We prayed some more. Then, she saw light. As we continued praying, she said she could make out forms. Finally, we brought her husband around in front of her. You should have seen the look on her face as she said, "I see my husband!" She was healed.

The Commission for Healing

Every one of us, as a Christian, has a commission from the Lord to pray for and to be used in healing the sick. It is not just for the elders of the church. When James wrote of the sick calling for the elders of the church (see Jas. 5:14-15), I believe he was referring to a situation where the sick person was unable to go to the gathering of God's people. The elders, then, who often were devoted full-time to the Lord's service, would go to the sick person to anoint him and pray for healing. Everyone in the church has the same commission. Listen to Jesus' words in Matthew:

> *As you go, preach this message: "The kingdom of heaven is near." Heal the sick, raise the dead, cleanse those who have leprosy, drive out demons. Freely you have received, freely give* (Matthew 10:7-8).

We are commissioned to heal. Someone may object and say, "Wait a minute. That's not sound interpretation. Jesus spoke this to His disciples. We can't apply to every believer what Jesus spoke only to His disciples." My response is, "Okay, but Jesus said an awful lot to His disciples. If we cut out everything He said to them as not applying to us, we wouldn't have much of the Gospels left." My point still stands. We all have a commission from Him to heal.

Mark 6, verses 7 and 13, says, "Calling the Twelve to Him, He sent them out two by two and gave them authority over evil spirits. ... They drove out many demons and anointed many sick people with oil and healed them." Notice how prominent deliverance, the casting out of devils, is in the commissioning. Now some would say, "This is still directed only to Jesus' disciples."

Consider the words of Jesus that are known as the Great Commission:

Therefore go and make disciples of all nations, bap-
tizing them in the name of the Father and of the Son
and of the Holy Spirit, and **teaching them to obey**
everything I have commanded you. *And surely I am*
with you always, to the very end of the age (Matthew
28:19-20).

Once again, Jesus is speaking to His disciples:
"Therefore go and make disciples of all nations, bap-
tizing *them*...and teaching *them* to obey everything I
have commanded you." Who does Jesus mean by *them*?
Now He is clearly moving beyond His own disciples to
future generations of believers, which include *us*. The
commission to obey everything Jesus has commanded
includes us. As believers, we have been anointed and
commissioned by the Lord to obey His commands. Part
of that obedience is to evangelize the lost and pray for
the sick.

The Scope of Healing

Once we answer the question of whether or not God
still heals today, another question arises: To what extent
does God heal? How wide is the scope for healing?
There are some people who have a very narrow view
on divine healing today; they believe God can heal
headaches but not cancer; physical illness but not mental
illness. It is one thing to believe intellectually that God
can heal, but quite another to actually expect Him to do
it right now, right where we are. It is the difference
between *head* faith and *heart* faith; between mental

assent to a principle and expectancy based on the power, the purpose, and the promises of God.

What is the scope of healing? Psalm 103 gives us an idea:

> *Praise the Lord, O my soul; all my inmost being, praise His holy name. Praise the Lord, O my soul, and forget not all His benefits—who forgives all your sins and heals all your diseases* (Psalm 103:1-3).

These verses reveal a comprehensive scope; the word *all* occurs four times. The Lord forgives *all* our sins. Does God still forgive sins today? Of course He does. (I certainly hope so!) Does He forgive *all* our sins? Yes. The Lord heals *all* our diseases. Does God still heal today? Yes. Forgiveness of sins and healing of diseases are listed together here. If one is true today (forgiveness), why wouldn't the other one (healing) be true as well? God can forgive all our sins, yet not everyone in the world receives forgiveness. It depends on the conviction of sin in a person's heart by the Holy Spirit, and that person's response to that conviction. In the same way, God can heal all our diseases, yet not everyone gets healed. I don't know why.

The point is, the scope of God's healing includes every type of disease. Nothing is excluded. It is as easy for God to heal cancer as to heal a toothache. The power to heal does not lie in us; it is in God alone. The question is, do we have enough faith to *pray* for that kind of healing? Faith for healing is not faith in us, but faith in God. If we have the faith to pray, and God shows up and heals, then we can simply bless what He does.

Once in Toronto I prayed for a 14-year-old girl named Heather who had dyslexia. I had prayed for her earlier, and she and her family returned for more prayer after the main ministry time was over. The first time I had prayed, she had fallen out in the Spirit, shaking for awhile. The second time she fell out again, but lay very still for quite some time. When she got up she said she had felt cold, like her body temperature was dropping. Heather described a vision in which she had been lying on an operating table while angels opened up her head, rewired her brain, and put it back together. This was several years ago. I have checked with her every year since then, and she is still free of dyslexia.

Heather went home and visited her best friend, Monica, who also had dyslexia. Without saying anything about her vision she told Monica, "Jesus is going to heal you." Heather put her hands on Monica's head, and Monica went out. Monica too had a vision of angels operating on her head and rewiring it, and was totally healed of her dyslexia.

The Basis of Healing

The biblical basis for healing is linked to three important scriptural themes: the covenant relationship, the atonement of Christ, and the Kingdom of God.

Concerning the covenant relationship, the Book of Exodus says:

> *Then the Lord said: "I am making a covenant with you. Before all your people I will do wonders never before done in any nation in all the world. The people you live among will see how awesome is the work that I, the Lord, will do for you"* (Exodus 34:10).

The word *wonders* means miraculous things in nature. It also refers to miraculous things done in the hearts and bodies of the people: signs and wonders, which is another way of saying healings and deliverances.

So healing is part of God's earliest covenant with Israel. As the Church, the Body of Christ, we have the new covenant that God has written on our hearts (see Jer. 31:31-33). The Book of Hebrews says that we have a new and better covenant based upon a better sacrifice (Jesus) with better promises (see Heb. 7:22). If healing was in the old covenant, then it certainly is in the new and better covenant.

Healing is also linked to the atonement of Christ:

> *Surely He took up our infirmities and carried our sorrows, yet we considered Him stricken by God, smitten by Him, and afflicted. But He was pierced for our transgressions, He was crushed for our iniquities; the punishment that brought us peace was upon Him, and by His wounds we are healed* (Isaiah 53:4-5).

The Hebrew word translated "sorrows" in verse 4 can also be translated as "diseases." Matthew makes direct reference to this verse in connection with Jesus' healing the sick:

> When evening came, many who were demon-possessed were brought to Him, and He drove out the spirits with a word and healed all the sick. This was to fulfill what was spoken through the prophet Isaiah: "He took up our infirmities and carried our diseases" (Matthew 8:16-17).

Healing is part of the atoning work of Christ. Everything we receive from God comes by His grace and mercy, through the cross upon which His only begotten Son died. Because of the atonement of Christ, we receive the grace of God instead of His judgment. Healing is part of that grace.

A third biblical basis for healing is the Kingdom of God itself. Luke records the time when Jesus commissioned 72 disciples and sent them in pairs ahead of Him to prepare the towns and villages for His visit. He gave them instructions on how to act and what to do, part of which was, "Heal the sick who are there and tell them, 'The kingdom of God is near you' " (Lk. 10:9). There is healing in the Kingdom of God. That Kingdom is both now and "not yet," which is why not everyone gets healed now. The Bible makes it clear that there will be no pain, sorrow, or disease in Heaven, after the Kingdom has fully come, but that full consummation must await the Second Coming of Christ. The time when everyone will be healed has not arrived, so until then there will be ebb and flow, with occasional and increasing "breaking in" of the Kingdom.

There is a danger of misunderstanding here. In Luke 10:9 Jesus says, "The kingdom of God is near you"; in Luke 17:21 He says, in part, "...the kingdom of God is within you." The danger is that we could logically deduce that if the Kingdom of God is in us, and healing is in the Kingdom, then healing is in *us*, and *we* can heal people. That may be logical, but it is not biblical. The power for healing is never in *us*, but in the Lord who abides in us. It is God who heals, not us.

Chapter 3 of the Book of Acts tells the story of the man crippled from birth who was healed by God's power through Peter. The crippled man begged for alms every day at the temple gate called Beautiful. One day he called out to Peter and John as they were passing by and asked them for money. Peter looked at the man and said, "Silver or gold I do not have, but what I have I give you. In the name of Jesus Christ of Nazareth, walk" (Acts 3:6). Peter helped the man up, his feet and ankles were strengthened instantly, and he went with them into the temple courts, leaping and praising God. A crowd quickly gathered, amazed to see walking the man all of them knew had been crippled from birth.

Peter could have said, "You should have seen me! I had a powerful word of knowledge that was so strong that the power of God just flew through me." He could have brought the attention on himself. Instead, he focused the attention squarely on God:

> …*"Men of Israel, why does this surprise you? Why do you stare at us as if by our own power or godliness we had made this man walk? … By faith in the name of Jesus, this man whom you see and know was made strong. It is Jesus' name and the faith that comes through Him that has given this complete healing to him, as you can all see"* (Acts 3:12,16).

Peter was the first Teflon® Christian. Teflon® is a non-stick surface. Whenever praise or glory came Peter's way, he did not let it stick to him, but pointed beyond himself to the One who really did the healing. We need to be Teflon® Christians too. When the praise and the glory come when God shows up, we must not let it stick to us, but give it all to the Lord.

The Great Commission of Matthew 28:19-20 is for all of us. We are to obey *everything* Jesus has taught us. It is incumbent upon us to share our faith, pray for the sick, and learn how to cast out demons. That is the basic gospel; none of it is peripheral.

The Motive for Healing

There are many good and positive motives for wanting to see people healed: compassion for the sick, love of people, desire to see someone free of pain. There is one motive for healing, however, that I believe God delights to bless more than any other, and it is found in the Book of Acts:

...and the name of the Lord Jesus was held in high honor (Acts 19:17).

Whether we are praying for healing, celebrating in worship, or proclaiming the gospel to the lost, our central focus should be exalting the Lord Jesus Christ and holding His name in high honor. When we do so, God is pleased and responds to our prayers and moves in our midst.

Chapter 8

Bill and Barbara Cassada: From Air Traffic Control to Global Awakening

Why would anyone give up $150,000 a year to work full-time as unpaid volunteers with an itinerant international ministry? Ask Bill and Barbara Cassada. Since July 1997 they have traveled with me, coordinating the administrative details, conducting ministry team training in healing prayer and deliverance, and participating actively in ministry. Prior to this, they both held lucrative, high-level management positions with the federal government in air traffic control. Bill left his job first, taking early retirement in 1995. Barbara followed in January 1997, walking away from $85,000 a year just six years short of retirement. Some people might say it sounds crazy, but Bill and Barbara wouldn't have it any other way. God has called them so profoundly, and they have seen Him work so powerfully in their lives and in the lives of others, that Bill says, "We wouldn't trade it. We wouldn't turn around and go back for anything."

Such a move was quite a step of faith for both of them, but the transition was a particularly significant adjustment for Barbara:

> I've worked hard all my life to be independent. It was important to me not to depend on anyone for anything. When I left my management job with the government, which was a pretty high position, especially for a woman, I had already waived any retirement benefits from Bill. We both expected that I could live on my retirement if anything happened to him. Leaving six years short of retirement was a major emotional adjustment for me because now, if anything happens to Bill, I have no income at all. I have to rely totally on God as my provider. He stripped away that independent mind-set in me and told me, "You are not independent. You are totally dependent on Me." He has given me a peace about it, though.

Bill and Barbara first became involved in the renewal in November 1994 when, on the advice of their pastor, they attended a prophetic conference at the Toronto Airport Christian Fellowship and were "pretty well zapped," as Bill says. Returning home to New Jersey, their pastor asked them to take charge of training ministry teams in preparation for a series of meetings I would be holding in Millville, New Jersey, in March 1995. That is where we met for the first time.

After that first meeting, Bill and Barbara gradually became more and more involved in the renewal in general and my ministry in particular. They helped administrate the "Thirty-One Days Around Jesus" meetings in Philadelphia in October 1996. They also received deliverance training in Philadelphia from the Argentinian Christian leaders Pablo Bottari, Dr. Pablo Deiros, and others, who have been involved in deliverance ministry for years. Bill and Barbara have since entered into a ministry of teaching others about deliverance ministry, working in that area often during our meetings. They have been with me in South Africa, Chile, Guatemala, Argentina, and Australia, as well as many places in the United States.

God Shows Up in Groton

Barbara remembers one particular night during a series of meetings at a church in Groton, Connecticut, when the Presence of God was more powerful and real than she had ever felt before:

> This particular night I was very tired, and Bill and I were sitting in the balcony. I had a fatigue headache that was just off the wall. Bill asked if I wanted to go back to the hotel, but I told him I wanted to wait for a little while and see how things went.

All of a sudden Randy began to pray. He said, "Come, Holy Spirit," and when he did, my headache immediately was gone. I sat up and looked at Bill and said, "He's going to need us." We both hit the stairs and went down to the third step from the bottom so Randy could see us from the platform.

It was then that I heard the sound—not quite a "mighty rushing wind," but rather a wail from many of the 600 people in the auditorium. It began from the back of the room and rolled forward with such intensity of power that when Randy motioned for us to come quickly, we reached the platform just ahead of a whole wave of people who ran to the altar. Randy, Bill, and I stood there looking at each other as if afraid that touching anyone would be like touching a live wire.

The pastor's son, who was also a pastor, told me afterwards, "I always wondered because of my curiosity if I would be the one standing up and looking around when God came in power and everyone else was on their faces. Just before He came, though, the Lord spoke to my heart and said, 'Get on the carpet, I'm coming.' I fell on my face and for an hour and a half was afraid to pick my head up and look around." His sister said that she was standing with her eyes closed and was afraid to look around for fear of being turned into a pillar of salt.

That's how powerful the Presence of God was in that place. I had never experienced it before and I was terrified, yet I didn't want it to stop. That night I reached a new level of understanding of the fear of the Lord. There wasn't a person in that room who wasn't scared. There were even people still in their seats unable to come forward from whom demons came out screaming; other people were healed. It went on for hours. It was absolutely awesome. I will never forget that night as long as I live.

Baptists Blasted in South Africa

Bill and Barbara have been witnesses and participants in some incredibly powerful movements of God's Spirit since they began traveling with me a year ago. One such visitation took place during our visit to South Africa in October 1997. That entire trip was one great time after another in the Spirit. God really moved in a wonderful way everywhere we went. People were just so hungry for more of God. One example is the Quigney Baptist Church in East London, the largest Baptist church in South Africa. On April 27, 1997, pastor Dave Gernetsky told his congregation, "From this point forward the Third Person of the Holy Trinity, the Person of the Holy Spirit of God, is welcome at this church." They were serious in their desire for a move of God, and God did not disappoint them. Bill describes what happened on the last night we were there:

> Barbara and I were tending to "last night" duties, a familiar routine for us while on the road with Randy: posting testimonies to our prayer network and taking inventory of and packing up the books and tapes. We were almost ready to rejoin the service where Randy was preaching when I heard a loud commotion.
>
> Stepping into the overflow room I saw that hundreds of people had come forward and were jammed elbow to elbow

around the platform and steps. The simple act of preaching had drawn them from their seats. They had come to repent, to worship, to give their hearts to the Lord, filling the aisles as even more came from the balcony. All were on their knees crying and praising God. Randy stopped preaching and simply prayed, "Come, Holy Spirit. I bless what You are doing here. Come and touch Your people."

The Holy Spirit of God fell on this packed-out Baptist church of over 2,500 worshipers, and all over the sanctuary people began to fall, to weep, and to shake. They fell over the backs of pews and into the aisles. Young and old; men, women, and children crowded the platform and climbed the steps. God was touching people all over the room.

Barbara and I made our way to the platform, a trip that required 20 minutes because of the mass of people laid out everywhere around us. We began laying hands on people, simply blessing the work of the Spirit. When we finally reached Randy, I asked him how he was doing. "I'm scared," he said. "I've never seen anything like this."

I looked around from the platform. Some of the people were in Holy Ghost ecstasy. Others were just plain scared. Their paradigms were being shattered; they had no place to put what they were seeing. God had shown up and was doing exactly as He pleased, without any help from us.

Randy has said that if all that ever happens is that people fall down, then we might as well all be home with our families. However, we continue to see countless lives changed after these visitations: people healed, delivered, set on fire for God, going to the mission field; people old and young stirred with a passion for the things of God. Truly, God is visiting His people.

Stepping Out of the Boat

In February 1998 we went to Australia and held meetings in Perth, Sydney, and Canberra, the capital city. Once again, God showed up and blessed His people in a mighty way. One remarkable feature of the meetings in Canberra is that they were hosted by the St. Thomas the Apostle Roman Catholic Church. The priest, Father Greg Beath, and a parishioner had visited Toronto in October 1997 and were completely "blasted" by the Holy Spirit. In November, John and Carol Arnott visited Father Beath's church in Canberra. God unzipped Heaven and the Holy Spirit fell. Renewal broke out in this Catholic church and continues to burn brightly. Even more remarkable is the fact that an Anglican church, an Assembly of God church, a Baptist church, and a Bible college joined together with this Catholic church for renewal meetings.

Bill and Barbara were in charge of training ministry teams at St. Thomas the Apostle in advance of our meetings there. One experience from this training illustrates how God uses a "little ole me." Bill relates the story:

> Our ministry team training is laid out in three basic parts: General Prayer Ministry, Prayer for Healing, and Prayer for Deliverance. As Barbara and I sat inside this Roman Catholic church with a worship team from a local Assembly of God church, I was reviewing my notes in preparation for teaching. Normally I conduct the training very methodically, but this day I felt the Lord leading me in a different direction. I sensed that God wanted me to teach on praying for the sick and specifically about words of knowledge. In addition, I felt

strongly that God wanted me to do the exercise that Randy does, where he asks God to give words of knowledge for healing to those who have never given one publicly before.

Now this was a huge step of faith for me. I've seen Randy do it hundreds of times, but I had never done it myself. Nevertheless, I taught the five-step healing prayer model, then about words of knowledge, what they were and how to recognize them. When I asked for those who had never given a public word of knowledge before, about 50 people raised their hands. I prayed, asking the Holy Spirit to give words of knowledge, then sat down on the platform and waited two minutes, the way Randy does.

At the end of the two minutes I asked, "Who believes they have a word of knowledge for healing?" At least 35 people raised their hands! As these people came forward and shared their words, I was amazed at the detail and accuracy of some of them. As the words of knowledge were shared, people with those conditions came forward and were prayed for by the person who had given that specific word. Very soon we began to get reports of healings. It was amazing to watch God work.

I had stepped out of the boat big time, and God had indeed used "little ole me."

Deliverance Down Under

Another example of God's using "little ole me's" involves deliverance during our Australia trip. As Bill tells the story:

On Thursday night we taught on the ministry of deliverance. Barbara began by explaining how deliverance and the setting free of captives is the Father's heart, then I taught what deliverance ministry is and what it is not. We followed this with the ten-step prayer model that we learned from the Argentinians.

Afterwards, I gave an altar call for those who wanted to receive prayer for strongholds of sin in their lives or for compulsive behaviors they could not get rid of. The altar call was very specific: any manifestations such as falling, weeping, etc., would be considered signs that God was bringing darkness to the surface, and anyone who came forward would be taken to a private place for prayer. (These manifestations are interpreted as demonic only during this prayer for deliverence.)

I waited. It was a defining moment, because at first no one stirred. I thought, *Okay, Lord, now what do we do?* Finally, one person came forward, assisted by a friend. Then two others came. I realized the courage it took for them to do this in front of everyone, and the total trust they were putting in us, as well as our responsibility to pray properly for them and treat them with love and respect. Then the floodgate opened, and at least half of those present came forward for prayer!

Barbara prayed the very confrontational in-the-face-of-the-devil-coming-against-evil-spirits prayers, and a few people began to sob and shake. We quickly hooked them up with members of the prayer ministry team and got them off to the prayer room. Before long, the ministry team resources were exhausted, and Barbara and I ended up ministering in the deliverance room ourselves. There were quite a number of people set free that night.

Ordinary Folks

Despite the countless people they have prayed over for healing and deliverance, and regardless of the powerful ways God has used them and continues to use them, Bill and Barbara Cassada insist that they are not special people. Bill says:

> We are about as ordinary as they come. There is no special qualification that we possess to be doing what we are doing; it is something that God has put together. All we did was say, "Okay, God, we'll do it." Anyone can do what we do if they want to.

Barbara adds:

> I don't have a college education, yet many people, even pastors, look to me for mentoring. Bill and I end up praying for more pastors than we do laypeople. We are just "little ole me's": air traffic controllers whom God has chosen to be involved in global awakening. We are just ordinary folks. That's the great power behind the current renewal: God is taking ordinary "little ole me's" and using them to do extraordinary things. If He can use us, He can use anybody.

Chapter 9

Michael Ellis: One Incredible Adventure

The last three years have been one incredible adventure for me. After I was baptized in the Holy Spirit in 1974, God began telling me that I was going to travel all over the world. For the next 20 years the only times I left Georgia were for occasional vacations to Florida or someplace like that. I never went anywhere as far as ministry was concerned. When the "fullness of time" came, as soon as I met Randy Clark, the next thing I knew I was traveling all over the country and all over the world. I did nothing to make it happen. It is a testimony to the faithfulness of God. When He says He is going to do something, He does it.

I first met Michael Ellis in December 1994, during meetings I was holding at the Atlanta Vineyard Christian Fellowship. This Christian businessman has been in land development all his professional life, and incorporated in his own business since 1979. For 20 years he has also been involved in the Christian counseling and deliverance ministries. Michael says he stumbled into it:

> When I entered the Charismatic movement, I was in my 20's, and still very young spiritually. I discovered early on that when I was in a group and began to pray, all of a sudden I would know what spirit was bothering someone, and that person would get released when I prayed for him. It seemed accidental at first. Finally, the Lord told me He was calling me into that ministry. At the time my wife and I were Baptists, and she was not sure about the Charismatic movement yet. I considered it further confirmation from God when she told me on the way home from a meeting one day that she felt we were called to a deliverance ministry. In 1990, I went through (John) Sandford's school on inner healing. Then I put it all together and now basically do inner healing and deliverance together.

Skeptic Converted

Michael went to Toronto in November of 1994 as part of a group of 12 from his church that included his pastor and Tommy, his friend of 20 years. Admittedly, Michael went as a skeptic. His long experience in counseling and deliverance made him especially suspicious of the unusual manifestations he saw at Toronto. He was disappointed with the first meeting. It seemed uninspired to him. Even when he was prayed for during ministry time and went down he felt no major presence of the Spirit. After just a few minutes he got up, thinking he had given in to the power of suggestion.

By the second night, Michael and Tommy had talked themselves into the conclusion that the whole thing was not of God. Michael wasn't interested in being prayed for that night. He just stood against the wall at the back and watched. Then something began to change. As Michael remembers:

> During the service, people were given the opportunity to share testimonies of what God was doing in their lives after receiving prayer at the meetings. My experience as a counselor had given me skill at discerning people's hearts and whether or not they were acting out of the flesh. These testimonies began to touch me. I could not deny them; they were real. God had deeply touched these people. One man from England spoke of a 20-year bondage broken by the Holy Spirit. Another from Australia had been on the verge of giving up on his church and ministry, but now was more excited than ever about the Lord and ready to take it back to Australia.

> The next day was rainy and cold, so we stayed in the hotel. Around 11:00 Tommy and I started praying, asking God what He was doing. During prayer we repented of our bad attitudes and God began to reveal some things in our lives. After some strongholds were broken in Tommy's life, he

began to laugh. As I had seen others at the meeting do, I waved my hand at him and said, "More." Tommy laughed louder. At that moment, I began to understand better what the Lord was doing. Then from deep in my spirit like a volcano erupting, a burst of joy exploded out of me. We laughed and cried together for the next two or three hours. We also saw many visions from the Lord.

One vision God gave me concerned Tommy's granddaughter, Sarah, who was seven at the time. She was worshiping the Lord with her hands lifted up. I told Tommy that she was not copying her parents, but worshiping on her own.

On Sunday morning I asked John Arnott to pray for us as a group before we returned home. I served as the catcher. When John prayed for Tommy, Tommy went down and *out*. When he woke up he shared a vision he had received of Sarah worshiping God before thousands of people. We rejoiced in the belief that God was really going to use Sarah.

On the plane home I pulled from my briefcase a book I had tossed in before leaving for Toronto: *Harvest II* by Rick Joyner. I turned to a chapter entitled "The Joy of the Lord" and was amazed to find the renewal phenomenon of "holy laughter" referred to as the "sign of Sarah," who laughed when she was told by the Lord that she would have a son, Isaac, whose name means "laughter." The author said it was time for the Church to give birth to "Isaac," the child of promise that will be the last-day ministry. What a powerful confirmation from God in connection with the visions Tommy and I had received!

When we returned from Toronto, everyone wanted to know what had happened to us. We went to church meetings and home groups, giving our testimonies, laying hands on people, and praying. The results were the same as we had experienced in Toronto. These truly are times of refreshing!

Letter of Recommendation

During 1995, Michael traveled extensively with me both at home and abroad assisting with the prayer and deliverance ministries. God orchestrated an interesting series of events to bring this about. It began the month after Michael returned from Toronto, when he attended the meetings I was doing at the Atlanta Vineyard. We met one evening and had a good time talking about our common Baptist roots. Michael recalls what happened the last night of the conference:

The Lord spoke to me in the middle of the service and said, "I want you to go with Randy; travel with him for a year and serve him, and then you will go out on your own." I dismissed it at first as being my own thoughts rather than God's. When the prayer ministry time came, Randy gave an invitation first to all who wanted to be missionaries, then a second one for any who wanted to go on missionary journeys. I had always wanted to do that, so I went forward. I felt that if Randy had started this thing in Toronto, then I wanted him to pray for me and I wanted double the anointing he had.

I had a tough time getting close to Randy. I stood in the back of the group for a long time, then when a hole opened up close to the front, my friend and I moved up. We were behind a couple being prayed for by Randy, when suddenly, we had to become the catchers. My friend caught the woman as she fell out, but her husband was still standing. Randy saw me and said, "Keep praying for him." As I prayed, Randy moved off to another part of the church. Soon, other people asked me to pray for them. Before I knew it, it was midnight and I still hadn't gotten Randy to pray for me. When I finally got close to him at the back of the church, Randy's assistant told me that Randy was very tired after praying for two and a half hours, and asked me to pray for *him*. When I did, Randy fell out and was on the floor for about half an hour. The Lord said to me, "I have opened the door, now you walk through it."

When Randy got up, I told him what the Lord had said about my traveling with him. He looked surprised, but we talked about it. As it turned out, we both knew John Sandford, so Randy asked me to get a letter of recommendation. I told him I would, but inside I didn't really think it would be possible; John Sandford kept a very busy schedule and traveled all over the world. So, I put the whole thing out of my mind.

The week after Christmas, I visited Toronto again. On the second night, I was surprised to see John Sandford sitting on the front row! I went over to him and he remembered me. We had lunch together the following Saturday, New Year's Eve. There were no meetings that night, so he asked me and my friends to come to his hotel suite. He, his son, and some counselors had been praying for people all week, but had not had anyone pray for them. He asked us to do it. We spent two or three hours there praying, and afterwards, I asked John for a letter of recommendation. He wrote one out on the hotel stationery, and I gave it to Randy when I saw him in Charlotte, North Carolina, in January 1995. That's how I began traveling with Randy.

Breaking Bondage in Norway

Michael Ellis has a strong prophetic gifting that God has used on numerous occasions to make significant spiritual breakthroughs. One such occasion was in Norway in June 1995. We had been warned that Norwegian people receive, but rarely fall out or display manifestations, so we didn't really know what to expect that first night. In fact, throughout the service, things seemed rather tame. Nevertheless, when I gave the call for prayer, half or more of the church came forward. What happened next was rather amazing. According to Michael:

> The Norwegians are strong on control, and it is hard for them to receive because their guard is up and their hearts are not open. As we began to pray, there was such a fear in them that they began what we called the "Norwegian shuffle": walking backwards 10 or 15 feet trying to remain standing while we followed them, praying. Finally, I asked the pastor if he could help me understand what was happening. He explained that Norway was celebrating 1,000 years of Christianity in the country. Centuries earlier, the king of Norway had become a Christian and then decreed that anyone who did not convert would be put to death.
>
> I realized then that for generations of Norwegians, God and Christianity had been objects of fear rather than of love

and forgiveness. With this understanding I began praying without my interpreter, asking the Lord to forgive those who had bound these people in such fear, and to forgive the people for being so fearful. Then I began to bind any spirit of fear or control in them. All of a sudden, they began falling out, and we had many of the same manifestations we had seen all over the rest of the world. Even so, it was difficult. Some of the people still couldn't open up. There was a real breakthrough, though, once we got past that barrier of fear.

Reconciliation in Australia

When Michael's year of traveling with me was over, a door opened for him to begin traveling with John and Paula Sandford. It was a combining of the Sandfords' focus on inner healing with Michael's on renewal. One of the first trips Michael made with the Sandfords was to Australia and New Zealand in March 1996. Once again God used him in a pivotal way to make a breakthrough.

One of the places Michael and the Sandfords ministered at was a Roman Catholic church in Melbourne, Australia. Like many other Protestants, Michael had grown up hearing and believing some very negative things about the Roman Catholic Church. In Melbourne, he was involved in counseling during the day and with renewal meetings in the evenings. On the final night, Michael was participating in a liturgical practice called "passing the peace." He picks up the story:

We had already been told that the priest, Father Victor, was going to serve communion that night to everyone, not just to Catholics. That was stepping across the line for him. As we were passing the peace I realized that I couldn't partake of this communion because of the negative things I still had in my heart about the Catholic Church. So as he came by I said, "Father Victor, I need to repent on behalf of myself and my Protestant brothers, and the church I grew up in, for all the things we have said against the Catholic Church and all the things we have done against you." Father Victor didn't let it rest there. Instead, before communion he had me come to the front. He repented for the Catholics and I repented for the Protestants and we and the entire congregation began to worship. The roof came off. We worshiped in the Spirit for half an hour. It sounded like a company of thousands, even though there were only 550 people there.

We began with regular songs of praise, but then there came a wondrous "singing in the Spirit" where everyone sings in tongues to his own melody. It all blended together until it seemed like one glorious voice. It was the most beautiful sound you could ever hear. That night, many people came forward and many were laid out on the floor. The Lord's presence was absolutely overwhelming, and I think it was His way of acknowledging our need for reconciliation with each other.

The Big Picture

Michael says that since his incredible adventure began three years ago, his horizons have totally changed:

I have gone from a perspective that took in only my immediate surroundings, my church affiliation, and the people closest to me, to a greater global awareness. I have become cross-denominational because I have been in almost every kind of church: Anglican, Catholic, Mennonite, Evangelical Free, Lutheran—you name it. My whole view of church has completely changed. So has my view of God. Everything is different because I see the bigger picture now. God doesn't seem to care about all the differences of belief that we get caught up in. He crosses all the lines. The Holy Spirit goes wherever anyone invites Him to come. The big adventure is still going on.

It is so true when Randy says, "God can use little ole me." God's plan in these last days is to pour out His Spirit on all flesh and raise up a nameless, faceless generation in His Church. There will be no superstars to carry the bulk of the ministry and the anointing, but ordinary, everyday people of faith who are open to God and who believe that He will do what He says He will do. Randy does not come from a background that would normally produce someone who travels all over the world, yet there he is. As for myself, I was a nobody. No one had ever heard of me, and many people still haven't, but it still amazes me that God would open the door for someone like me to travel all over the world. I keep saying, "God, I don't believe this is happening. I can't believe I'm here." Yet, God is always looking for someone who is willing to let Him work, and then break out of the mold and go for it.

Chapter 10

Father Barry Burrus: Fire in the Midst of the Snow

Cleddie (Keith) asked me to share a testimony of what has happened with me, and I guess you might say I preached a little. Luke 12:49 was the verse I launched out with, where Jesus says, "I have come to bring fire on the earth, and how I wish it were already kindled!" I said that God wanted us to let His fire touch us. Afterwards Cleddie invited people with Catholic roots to come up for prayer. Quite a few responded. I prayed with them, along with others. Our prayer ministry lasted a couple of hours. It was a good time. God truly touched a number of people. There was a good turnout that night, despite the big snowstorm we had. Fire came in the midst of the snow.

How did a Roman Catholic priest end up in Cleddie Keith's Heritage Fellowship Church in Florence, Kentucky, on a snowy Friday night, speaking about the fire of God? For Father Barry Burrus, such circumstances are becoming commonplace. Since being touched himself by God's fire, he has embarked on an itinerant ministry in renewal and revival that has led to invitations to speak in Protestant churches as well as Catholic, both in the United States and overseas.

Father Barry grew up in the Christian Church denomination, then later became a Methodist. He was baptized in the Spirit in 1977 and entered the Charismatic renewal. His interest in the Catholic Church was sparked after reading a history of Christianity and realizing how little he knew about the Church. As he studied more, he felt the Spirit gradually leading him in that direction. In 1979 he took "full communion" with the Catholic Church. After a number of years as an active layman, he entered seminary at the Sacred Heart School of Theology near Milwaukee, Wisconsin, and was ordained to the priesthood in June 1993. After serving as a parish priest in Clarkville, Kentucky, for several years, he was assigned to Ashland, Kentucky, in June 1997, to a full-time ministry fostering renewal and revival work in the parish. He conducts retreats, prayer meetings, and other revival-related activities, and celebrates the sacraments on a regular basis, but is also free to travel anywhere in the world to promote renewal and revival.

Facedown in Florence

Father Barry's first direct contact with the "Toronto Blessing" came in January 1997 when he attended the first service of a series of meetings I did at the Heritage Fellowship, Cleddie Keith's church in Florence, Kentucky. He knew a little about the movement and about me from information he had picked up through correspondence and over the Internet since first hearing about Toronto in the fall of 1994. How he came to attend that meeting was, in his words, an "unexpected providential circumstance":

> I was staying overnight in Florence after a meeting regarding a charismatic seminar I was going to give later in the month. As I was driving to the post office in Florence to mail some letters, I noticed the sign out in front of Cleddie's church announcing revival services with Randy Clark. I wondered if it was the same Randy Clark I had heard of who was associated with the "Toronto Blessing." On my way back from the post office, I slipped into the church and picked up a brochure. Apparently it was the same Randy Clark, so I decided to come to the meeting. I came incognito, without my clerical collar.

> I absolutely loved the praise and worship, which lasted at least an hour. When Randy introduced this whole revival experience that I had read about, he impressed me with the gentleness of his delivery. From a pastoral standpoint he handled it quite well. All evening I felt completely comfortable with his approach and ministry style. When the first altar call

came, I responded and went to the front for prayer, where I saw a lot of manifestations. Some people were moaning; others were shaking, laughing, or crying. One woman in front of me was being delivered from evil spirits, and they gently took her to a back room. None of this blew me away, because I had read about the manifestations, but they got my attention.

Personally, I experienced a tremendous peace that was linked to a sincere repentance before God and a call to holiness; a strong desire in my heart to be holy because God wanted me to be holy. I ended up facedown on the floor, not because of the power of the Spirit, but by my own choice. It is the same posture priests adopt at ordination—a prostration before God. I had been consecrated that way, and I felt that God wanted me to live that out more, to be holy and to love Him with all my heart, soul, mind, and strength. There were no strong manifestations, although I did notice that over the next few days the peace continued and I had a stronger desire for prayer and to get into God's Word more.

I went back to my seat and continued to soak in God's Presence. My overall impression was of a Father who loves His children and responds when they cry out to Him. How could He not answer when they come before Him, asking for Him to touch them? I realized that the Father, in great power, tenderness, and love had reached down from His throne to touch, heal, and pour out His Spirit on His children. That really capped the evening for me.

Two weeks later, Father Barry led a seminar called "A New Life in the Spirit" at a Catholic church in Ashland, Kentucky. It was a Friday-Saturday event presenting the basic gospel message on the love of the Father, salvation in Jesus Christ, and the gift of the Holy Spirit, with an opportunity for people to receive prayer for a greater outpouring of the Holy Spirit or to be baptized in the Holy Spirit. He had led about 25 of these seminars previously, but the one in Ashland was different because the power of God came more openly and strongly than he had ever seen before. In fact, one man there began openly manifesting demonic influence, and after an hour of prayer by several people, including the pastor, the man was set free of several major addictions. This increase in both the manifested Presence of God and demonic manifestations was one of the first changes Father Barry noticed in his ministry after his experience in Florence.

Revival Masses

One of the main things that Father Barry does in his current ministry of renewal and revival is conducting what he calls a "revival mass": traditional Catholic liturgy combined with dynamic praise and worship, biblical preaching, and the manifested power of the Holy Spirit. He testifies that God led him into this particular ministry; it was totally unexpected. According to Father Barry:

> I went on vacation in Florida for two weeks in March 1997 and, while there, conducted a mass in an apartment in Delray Beach. There were 11 people there, including two youth. It lasted three hours. God's power came mightily, with people falling over in the Spirit, laughing. I was asked to stay an extra day, and the next night we had mass in another apartment,

and the same thing happened, except that God's power was even greater. I served communion and right afterward looked up and saw what appeared to be flames of fire resting on everyone's shoulders and covering their heads. The moment I saw it, I felt it myself. I had never seen anything like it before, nor have I since. God's fire had fallen upon us right in the middle of mass! For the next two weeks I was "spiritually intoxicated," which had never happened before either. I felt the overwhelming Presence of God for two weeks straight, and it was then that I began to sense God's purpose in it.

The people in Florida invited me back in April, and paid my way. Before I went, I met with my bishop and shared with him what had happened. In May I began to receive invitations to go other places, such as Dallas, Texas. My bishop and I were seeking to understand what God was doing, and I finally told him that I felt the Lord might be calling me into revival ministry. In the meantime, the pastor in Ashland had asked the bishop to station me there so I could bring the renewal work further into his parish. After I wrote a proposal and submitted it to my bishop, he gave me permission to enter the renewal and revival ministry full-time.

Father Barry describes a typical revival mass:

Normally I give a very short introduction right at the beginning, followed by at least 30 minutes of praise and worship, usually led by a local music ministry. Sometimes they are involved in Charismatic renewal, sometimes not. During that time I try to facilitate worship and praise with a few comments, singing myself, and encouraging people to be joyful in the Lord. Most of the time I give some background on the whole matter of raising hands. Many times the people,

Catholics especially, have never been to anything charismatic, so the whole phenomenon of people raising their hands seems strange. I let them know that it is certainly within Catholic tradition because at every mass the priest raises his hands during the prayers. Also, the Psalms and the New Testament talk about raising hands. I share my own experience of how I began. It is a little unusual at first, but usually by the time we have finished the worship people are loosened up, warmed up, and more prepared.

Then I begin the mass itself, which consists of the normal rites of the Catholic mass with all its parts. I try to inject a little more liveliness into the experience and usually preach (we call it giving a homily) after the Scripture readings. I will choose some aspect of the Scripture readings and then talk about the ministry of Jesus, how He is here today to give us life, to heal us, and to restore us. Then I try to prepare the people for the experience of being prayed with. Sometimes I pray right then; sometimes I wait until the mass is over, but I always pray with anyone who wants prayer. I just try to give a sense of what the Holy Spirit is saying for that crowd, for that assembly, for that moment. The Eucharist (communion) follows. Sometimes I invite people to share a prophetic word.

The Father's Love

Father Barry says that the most consistent thing he has experienced since he was touched in Florence is a continuing deep awareness of the profound love of the Father. He has experienced it himself and has seen others deeply touched by His love. The Lord is coming in power to show that He is real and that He is greater than the occult and all the other powers of darkness that so many people get trapped in. God wants us to see how loving and powerful He is.

Father Barry Burrus is truly a "little ole me." Five-and-a-half feet tall and basically joyful by disposition, he experiences a great deal of freedom in his worship and ministry:

> When I go out there is a lot of joy. I seem to hop around a lot and get excited. In fact, a fellow priest in Arkansas dubbed me "the short, hopping priest." There is just a great freedom and joy in ministry. I delight to see what God does when we get together.
>
> I never dreamed that anything like this would ever happen through me or my ministry. I am astounded at how all this has opened up so quickly. It is wonderful to see how God's Spirit is being poured out—His fire falling to touch people, to heal people, to let them know that He is real, not abstract, and that they can experience Him and receive His touch, His blessing, His healing, and His deliverance. So I just stand back and enjoy watching God touch people and thank Him for choosing to use me in this way. What is even more amazing is realizing what a sinner I am, and yet He still uses me. I am very thankful.

Chapter 11

Andrea Johns: Holy Spirit Road Trip

One man who was a fairly new Christian—only a few weeks old in the Lord—was in my salon. While I was cutting his hair he said, "I grabbed my wife's curling iron by mistake, and now my whole hand is burned." I looked at him and asked, "Do you believe Jesus can heal you?" He got nervous and started stuttering, then finally answered, "Yes, I believe that." So I said, "Let's ask Him," then prayed over his hand. When I finished cutting his hair, he stood up and said, "My hand is healed. It is completely healed." The next week he showed up at my home group and received prayer for some other medical problems he has. God has really ministered to him.

Such matter-of-fact miracles as this are not unusual in Andrea Johns' experience. She has learned over the years to listen to and follow the promptings of the Holy Spirit and, as a result, has seen Him do some wonderful things through her life. Andrea is a good friend of my assistants, Bill and Barbara Cassada, and she too was touched by God at meetings I was a part of in New Jersey and Philadelphia.

Although this New Jersey hairdresser is a genuine "little ole me," she is not a novice in ministry. For over 18 years she has hosted a weekly Bible study in her home where healings and, more recently, deliverances, have become almost commonplace. During that time she has seen the focus of the group change many times:

It started out with a strong evangelistic thrust because I was a new Christian and real enthusiastic. All I wanted was for all the people I used to hang out with in the bars to come to Christ, so I was inviting tons of people, and the new people were inviting new people, and it kept that focus for a few years. Then it seemed to change to a singles group for awhile, with a lot of single adults being filtered into the church through the Bible study. After that it became a discipleship group, focusing on nurturing Christian growth and biblical principles; then it swung back to an evangelistic group again. I have had a bevy of teachers over the years, including Bill Cassada, and almost everyone who has taught my home group has ended up in ministry as pastors, rescue mission people, even missionaries.

There is no greater joy than to watch all this happen. It has been an 18-year Holy Spirit road trip.

Aside from her home group, Andrea's base of operations is the beauty salon where she has worked for 20 years. Both her boss and her co-worker are Christians, and Andrea has great freedom there to minister in the name of Jesus. It is her mission field. Andrea says:

> My boss will point me out to a customer and say, "See that woman over there? She'll pray with you." Almost daily I take people into the bathrooms or the pedicure rooms and pray over them. I pray with them right in the shampoo bowl or in the chair. Not too long ago, a man we had prayed for, for 18 years, was saved. I was able to kneel down right in the front window and pray with him to receive Christ. My co-worker was with another Christian woman in the chair, doing her hair, and they were both praying for me while I ministered to this man. It was incredible.

The Road to Millville

Andrea met the Cassadas through the salon. Bill and Barbara at that time were backslidden Christians, drifting without any regular church involvement. Years earlier they had been burned by a brief, bad experience in ministry. The Lord gave Andrea a burden to pray for Barbara, and then for Bill, before she had even met him. Then one day God brought Bill into her beauty shop chair. As Andrea remembers:

> The Holy Spirit came over me in one of those moments when you speak in fear and trembling, and He began to speak

words to Bill through me. Bill didn't even know me yet. I hadn't been working on his head for five minutes when God took over and spoke the Scripture to Bill, "Simon, Simon, Satan has asked to sift you as wheat" (Lk. 22:31). I can remember it like it was yesterday. That's how scared I was. I just knew he would say something like, "Who do you think you are?" Instead, Bill went home and God led him to the Scriptures and transformed his heart.

Bill and Barbara had not found a church yet, so I begged them to come to my home group where they could be loved on and encouraged. God led them into a church, but they also got involved in my home group, and before long I felt the Lord lead me to ask Bill to teach the group. God has given me this ability to see people beyond where they are. It's a strange gift, but I seem to know their potential before they do. It's not me, but the Lord shows me what they are meant to be. I knew God was training Bill for something else. Bill taught the group for a number of months and he began to move into a place of influence in his church.

Eventually, Bill became involved with a group of pastors from Millville, New Jersey, who were sponsoring a series of meetings with Randy Clark. Bill shared with me about the meetings and how exciting they were, so I went. It was incredible.

A couple of things in particular touched Andrea at the Millville meetings: the spirit of ecumenical unity and her own refreshing from God. About these things Andrea says:

I was convinced God was there because I had never seen such unity among leadership: 25 pastors and their wives all being prayed for and the church filled with all different denominations. My home Bible study group has always focused on the Body of Christ, not denominations, so it was a dream come true to see denominational and racial barriers being destroyed and people coming together simply because they wanted to be in God's Presence.

Originally, I went to Millville as an observer, but I knew that I was not going to receive what I wanted from God unless I entered in. The Lord made it clear that in my case the only way to receive a blessing was for me to press in to God for what I wanted. Randy made the same thing clear in his message. I took it to heart and pressed in for Randy to pray for me. I wanted to know what it was like to be touched by the power of God. My legs caved in under me and I went down. I didn't see any visions or anything like that, but I did go home with a new and fresh touch from Jesus and a renewed hunger and thirst for more of Him. That night God began a great healing in my heart and spirit.

Healing and Deliverance

After her Millville experiences, Andrea began going to meetings and conferences whenever she could. She was able to attend only one day of the deliverance training given by the Argentinian leaders in Philadelphia, but received more thorough training in the deliverance model a few months later in Florence, Kentucky. Two things stand out for her from the Philadelphia conference. First, she witnessed Fred Grewe's deliverance of a pastor's wife from migraines and a spirit of fear (see Chapter 6), and second, she and a friend received deep inner healing through the prayer of one of the Argentinian pastors. According to Andrea:

> He was praying for my girlfriend through an interpreter, speaking to her things that only she and I and God knew—deep things from her past, truths that only God could speak through this man, through the interpreter, and right into her soul. God ministered such healing to her in my presence, and He let me hear it because it healed my soul too. I had been close to this woman for 17 years and knew her pain and her needs, and God touched her. Then this pastor came to me and began to speak the truth to my heart with prophetic words that only God and I knew. God touched me in a deep, beautiful turning-point way in my life.

Two significant things happened for Andrea in Florence, Kentucky, too: she received an impartation of the gift of intercession when an Argentinian pastor prayed for her, and her back was completely healed over a period of several weeks from pain due to arthritis. Since her impartation, God has led Andrea into a much deeper understanding of Holy Spirit intercession, and she has moved in that ministry to a greater degree than ever before.

When Andrea returned from Philadelphia she began to notice some changes in the spirit and tone of her home group:

There was a stirring of greater hunger for God. People were coming who were just wanting more and more of God. When God touches the hearts of the leaders, He also touches the hearts of the people at the same time. You are a cleaner vessel for the Spirit to flow through. The more you surrender the flesh, the more the Spirit flows. That's what started to happen. People would come and just pray. I couldn't shut them up; at midnight people would still be in my living room praying and fervently seeking God. It was amazing. At this point I wasn't seeing any great miracles. I saw the miracle of salvation on a regular basis, which was awesome enough in itself, but no unusual demonic manifestations or anything like that. I know it was because I really wasn't ready for it.

Once Andrea returned from Florence, Kentucky, however, things changed and she began to see demons manifest in her home group. It was rather awkward at first:

As these things began to happen, only the four of us who had been to Florence knew what was happening. One night a woman asked us to pray for her and as we did, she slumped over in a heap feeling faint and like she needed to throw up. We recognized from our training that this was a demonic manifestation, so two of us took her onto the back porch while the other two maintained decorum in the living room. We worked through the deliverance model that we had learned and God brought relief and freedom to this woman. As the weeks unfolded, this began to happen more in a very slow, one-by-one process in my group. On another night, an 18-year-old man was delivered from lust and other demonic strongholds in his life while "normal" things were going on in the living room.

Another change Andrea noticed in her home group was an increase in the number of healings. Most of the time, prayer for healing comes not in the group meeting itself, but at the back door as people are leaving. Different ones will ask her to pray for a pain or a sickness they have, and many times God heals them. Andrea shares a couple of examples:

> One girl said to me, "Ever since that night last fall that you prayed for my relationship with my boyfriend, and my heart condition, God has done miracles. I have since gotten married, my life and family have been transformed, and I haven't taken a single pill for my heart." A man asked me to pray for his hand. The next week he came back and said, "Last week you prayed for my hand and God healed it. Now, would you pray for my elbow?" I was standing at the back door praying for his elbow. He came back the next week and told me, "The first week you prayed for my hand and God healed it; the second week, you prayed for my elbow, and God healed it. This week pray for my shoulder." It was hilarious, but I did it just because he asked, not because I felt any great anointing upon me. Yet, God healed him. I realized that God was doing something in our midst.

Divine Appointments

Andrea shares about one day in her life recently where God's hand seemed to be all around her:

I had a bronchial infection or something and couldn't work. A girlfriend of mine was in the hospital. The Lord told me to go see her and gave me a Scripture and a prophetic word for her. On my way to the hospital, I had to stop at the gas station. The young man pumping my gas really looked miserable, and the Spirit prompted me to pray for him. At first I resisted, but finally asked the young man if I could pray. He gave me his hand and as I prayed about how much the Father loved him, and was bigger than all his problems, he sobbed his eyes out. It turned out that his fiancée had just broken up with him. After prayer, I asked him if he knew Jesus and he said yes. I told him then that God wanted him to know that He had not left him, and to trust Him. I saw the peace of God come over his face as he said, "I will."

When I got to the hospital and was walking up the sidewalk, there was an elderly black woman in front of me walking very slowly and painfully. The Spirit told me to pray for her. Again I resisted. I couldn't just go up to her and pray for her! She would think I was crazy! So I just said, "How are you?" "Not too good." I told her I was sorry and would pray for her, and kept walking. When I got inside I saw the wheelchairs and took one and offered to push the woman wherever she needed to go. She acted offended and told me she could manage. I told her that I hoped she felt better, then went on my merry way.

As I passed one office I saw a little fledging of mine from a Bible study I had started in an apartment complex in a really poor side of the tracks. This young woman had gotten saved at that Bible study. When she saw me she squealed with delight and said, "I can't believe you are here! I need you to pray for me right now." So I prayed for her through this Plexiglas window.

When I got back to the elevators to go see my girlfriend who I was originally supposed to visit anyway, there was the elderly black woman again! We both laughed, then I said to her, "Let's ride together. God wants me to pray for you." She got in the elevator and said, "All right. Push 'three' and pray for me." I prayed for her right there in the elevator even as other people were getting on.

I finally got to my girlfriend's room. She had been in the hospital for weeks and was really discouraged and depressed. I said to her, "Wait until I tell you why God has you in this hospital and what He's done because you are here, because if you weren't here, none of this would have happened." As I told her, she began praising God that there was a purpose in her illness.

Andrea shares this insight as a "little ole me":

One thing that God has made very clear to me is that I am unique and I should not model myself after any other person. God wants to do a unique thing in me because He is a unique God and the Holy Spirit has a unique ministry for each of His children. He wants to do His work in me for His time and His place and His moments. The Book of Acts, chapter 17, says that God knows the exact time and place where we live and move and have our being. In His uniqueness He will use me the way He wants to. All the ministries and examples that I have seen and learned from are designed to teach, encourage, and inspire me and touch my life so that God can use little ole me the way He wants to.

Chapter 12

Bob Bradbury: The Galilean Fisherman

God is raising up a generation of anointed kids. He is raising an army; kids are coming to these meetings, God is touching them, and they are signing up. Then God is turning them loose to go out and bring others in.

Bob Bradbury is in a position to know what he's talking about. Following in the footsteps of Peter, Andrew, James, and John, in 1994 this ex-sea captain traded his boats and fishing for a singularly effective outreach ministry to children and teenagers. Using a fishing net and the chrome steering wheel from an old fishing boat to show how God wants to use everyone in the church, Bob has reached hundreds of kids, including many who would not respond to a traditional altar call. Typically, in the prayer and ministry time that follows, God shows up and mightily touches the children and youth. Some fall, others shake; very few are left unaffected. Age doesn't seem to matter. Preschoolers are touched as readily as high school students. The children are encouraged to pray for others, and healings have resulted in some cases. In one way or another, almost all are touched.

Before being touched in Toronto and receiving his call to children's ministry, Bob was a successful entrepreneur in Rhode Island as a U.S. Coast Guard-licensed fishing captain with his own boat-building business. A licensed commercial instrument pilot, Bob also served the local fishing industry by doing fish spotting from his own plane. He gave it all up to follow the call of God in his life, walking away from $180,000 a year to go into churches of all different denominations and to people from all walks of life with the powerful message of the love of God and the saving grace of Jesus Christ.

Bob and his wife Susie traveled to Toronto in January 1994 because they heard that God was showing up and that the Holy Spirit was moving, and they wanted to see for themselves. Bob admits he didn't really want to be there, particularly after he saw what was going on:

> I was standing about ten feet from the rear door to get out of the place because I saw all these people jumping up

and down and having a good time. I didn't really think it was God. Then four teenagers came in, dirty and scruffy with soccer balls under their arms. I turned and said to Susie, "Can you imagine these people here allowing these children in like this?" When I turned back around and looked, they were already out under the power of the Holy Spirit, without anyone praying for them. It was just the Presence of God that touched them.

Randy gave an altar call and it seemed as though everyone there was touched except for me. The next day, Susie and I went to the afternoon meeting for missionaries, evangelists, and pastors. The room was packed. Everything was quiet and nothing much was happening when I was suddenly hit with the spirit of laughter so hard that I fell off my chair. It hit Susie too. We were the only two people in the room affected that way at that time.

Randy gave another altar call and I went forward to be one of the catchers. As Randy went by praying for people, he saw me and said, "Bless him, Father. Bless him, Jesus," and then I got hit and was on the floor like a tuna out of water. Now, I am a tough guy, a sea captain for 30 years, and no one could hold me to the floor if I didn't want to be there, yet now I couldn't get up. I was scared and started calling out, "Jesus, Jesus!" When I stopped, I saw a vision of Jesus in a white robe coming out of a cloud and putting His hand on my shoulder. Immediately I felt a surge like 220 volts of electricity through my body. That experience changed my life.

A Heart for the Children

A few months after his experience at Toronto, Bob attended a meeting I held at *The 700 Club* in Virginia Beach, Virginia. I gave an altar call for children, and Bob was one of the people who prayed for them. He recalls it vividly:

> There were hundreds of kids there and while I was among them I literally felt the impartation of the Holy Spirit come into my body, and I couldn't move, but just stood there weeping and crying for the children and the teenagers who came forward. I asked the Lord to bless the kids and prayed for them that they would go down under the touch of the Holy Spirit. The meetings went on for four days. I don't believe I got 12 hours of sleep during that time because we were praying for people in two meetings a day. Then I would go back to my room shaking from the anointing of God.

God opened up Bob's special ministry to children almost immediately after his return from Virginia Beach:

> I was in my home church and was praying for three boys when they all went out under the power of the Holy Spirit. Each of them had a vision of Jesus. They were under so long that their mothers were getting concerned. I got them up off the floor one at a time and interviewed them separately. Each of them had the same story: Jesus had come down, taken them by the hand, and they had gone for a walk. That's when I realized that the Lord wanted me to work with youngsters and teenagers.

It wasn't long before Bob began to receive invitations to lead meetings for children and youth. The first one he did was at the Cathedral of St. Peter and Paul, a Roman Catholic church in Providence, Rhode Island, with around 45 kids present. Since 1994 his ministry has grown, and today he is on the road about 18 days a month. The meetings are normally on weekends, Friday through Sunday, but often carry over. This is a totally God-directed ministry. The size of the church, the location, the denomination, or the number of people expected mean nothing to Bob. He goes where the Lord leads him.

Bob Bradbury's ministry is not limited to church meetings, however. Since he began, his approach has expanded to where the common pattern is to go into a housing area, often a poor area such as "Section Eight" subsidized housing, and draw the kids together with worship music. Then he gives out permission slips, and those children who receive their parents' permission are bused to the meeting site the following night. He even involves children from the host church in this outreach. This approach is inspired by Bob's vision of the Great Commission of Matthew 28:19-20:

> It's more than going in and having a party; it's incorporating Matthew 28 through evangelism and bringing these kids into the church. That's where I am seeing the greatest anointing. It is when we are not only having meetings, but incorporating what God wants to do through the visions that He has

shown me. It's not like He sends me a television production; all I do is follow the peace that the Lord puts in my heart.

As to the focus of his message, Bob says:

I teach on the Great Commission from Matthew 28, the Galilean fisherman teaching model, and the message that "God can use little ole me": He can use the foolish things of the world to confuse the wise, and the weak things of the world to pull down the things that are mighty. Most of my talks are on service, that the anointing is for servanthood. That's my heart: empowering the kids and then releasing them to go out and do it. That's also what draws people in.

We may go into a church the first night with 30 kids and tell them what God is doing throughout the world. Then God touches them, anoints them, imparts to them, and then they go out and bring in their friends, and maybe even some who aren't their friends, and God touches *them*. Then those go out for others, and you know what that produces? Revival. We have seen skinheads, drug pushers, all sorts of people come to the Lord this way. That's what He is doing right now.

The Cross and the Commission

Bob Bradbury's drive to teach and model the Great Commission in his ministry was nailed home to him through a unique sign he received from the Lord. Bob lives near the University of Rhode Island and often exercises there by walking several miles. It was on one of those walks that the Lord spoke to him. According to Bob:

The University of Rhode Island has one department that develops lawn seed, and they have these massive green fields that are all beautifully groomed. They are all green. I was walking there one day shortly after all this began in my life—Toronto, Virginia Beach, and such—and I was asking the Lord, "What is this all about?" For awhile He said nothing, but after about a quarter of a mile the Lord said, "Stop." So I stopped, looked over to my left, and thought I saw something in the grass. I walked over to it, about 100 feet, and it was a big cross, maybe 20 feet long, burned and brown right in the middle of that green grass. I ran home, got my camera, and took a picture of it. Two days later it was gone; bright green grass covered the spot where it had been. When I saw the cross I just started weeping. I thought of how Jesus went up on the cross for us for the forgiveness of sin. An instant later came the thought of the Great Commission in Matthew 28.

When we have ministry with these kids, I tell them, "God really loves you and He wants to use you." In all my teachings I talk about Matthew 28, the Great Commission; that it is more than just an in-house church party and that God wants us to take the gospel to the nations. With the kids, however, the "nation" is right outside the church door. Their nation is their neighborhood. If they go into those neighborhoods and pray that the Lord would bring forth fruit, then God is going to do that. I try to give them an education and impartation of what the Lord showed me.

I start every meeting with a prayer for the Holy Spirit to come, then we give honor and praise to the Lord. After that I say, "Don't sit down. Put your hand on your head and repeat after me, 'God can use little ole me.'"

Chapter 13

Rick and Annie Stivers: Through Open Doors

I think that God, over these last few years, has shown us that when we rest in Him every day, He is faithful in opening doors. When we went to Russia the first time, we had absolutely no idea why we were going. We felt that God was drawing us there, even during a time when missionaries were being sent home because of everything that was going on in Russia. The greatest thing we learned is that when we are obedient to what God says, He will be our protection and He will make a way, no matter how impossible it seems. There were obstacles to overcome in Russia, and there still are, but I believe that God still has a purpose there, and we have seen some of that. It has been awesome to see God's faithfulness in doing the impossible.

Such a forward-looking and confident dependence on God is evidence of the changes that have occurred in the lives of Annie Stivers, her husband Rick, and their children since they were caught up in the renewal in the spring of 1995. How that came about, and what happened during the first year or so afterward, are detailed in Rick's book, *We Caught the Fire and Our Britches Are Still Burning*. Since that book is readily available, my focus in this chapter will be on what has happened in their lives since 1996.

By their own description, the Stivers were your average American Christian family. Rick's life revolved around his successful insurance business; Annie was a stay-at-home mom caught up with home-schooling their four children and with trying to achieve what she thought a Christian family should look like. As Annie says, "We loved the Lord, but He was only a part of our lives; we hadn't really allowed Him to be everything, or to let our lives revolve around His plans and desires."

Rick and Annie went to Toronto in May 1995, where Annie was touched significantly. Rick, however, experienced nothing visible or tangible. It was on the flight home that he first noticed a change. Before leaving for Toronto, Rick had negotiated a deal on a brand-new $50,000 Cadillac, which was a big step for him.

Unsure of what might happen in Toronto, he decided to wait until he got back to finish the deal. He thought it might turn out to be the wrong step. As Rick remembers:

> During the trip home the Lord started to speak to me. That's when I really began to accept the Presence of the Lord. One of the things He told me was, "Don't forget that I have plans for you in the upcoming months and years. You don't need to be getting into a big Cadillac right now." So, I didn't get my Cadillac.

Annie changed in noticeable ways too:

> In a nutshell, when I came home it took me five days to unpack, and that was a witness to my sister-in-law that this was God. I was a very organized and orderly person. I would make the family unpack even if we got home at midnight. I wanted everything in our home in order and under control. After Toronto was probably the first time in my whole life that I really gave God control of my life and let Him come and love me. I was very much into doing instead of being and letting the Lord love me for who I am. It was a very drastic change.

"Catch the Fire," Moscow, 1997

Annie and Rick first met me in Pasadena in October 1995. God had already spoken to them about going to Russia, and they came to Pasadena hoping to see me and talk about my plans for visiting Russia. We were in the midst of preparing for the first "Catch the Fire" conference in Moscow. Rick's book, *We Caught the Fire*, narrates in detail their six-month stay in Russia and the powerful move of God at that first conference. The Stivers returned to Moscow for the second "Catch the Fire" conference in 1997. Annie went over two months ahead of time with two other intercessors to help prepare through prayer for the conference. They had people all over the world praying.

The Lord gave Annie and others a strong burden and impression of what He wanted to do in Russia. As Annie describes it:

> We knew there would be a release of healing and forgiveness with regard to abortion. On the average, ten million babies a year are aborted in Russia. The average Russian woman has anywhere from 5 to 15 abortions in her lifetime. So we felt that this was going to be very significant. As it turned out, the conference dealt with a lot of inner healing and a lot of deliverance and there was a whole session on the issue of abortion. We saw women in their 60's and 70's who had struggled with guilt over this all their lives get free in the Lord. Many of them found expression for their joy in a new freedom in worship that was wonderful to see.
>
> Healing and deliverance occurred in a lot of the men as well, because abortion had involved them too. I think this was very significant because it was bringing healing to the nation. Everything about Russia is still very depressing and dark-oriented. There is still a lot of hopelessness. The inroads that this conference made against abortion and despair I believe is a further sign of the release of God's light and hope for the people of Russia.

Rick tells of an American missionary in northern Russia who traveled several days to attend the conference even though he was skeptical:

> He was one of those guys with every hair in place, very proper. Annie had organized teams of intercessors to intercede behind the stage during the meetings. On this particular night there was a lot of deliverance going on related to the abortion issue and the intercessor team for the night consisted of five or six children ranging in age from 9 to 13. These kids had such a burden of intercession that they were just wailing and weeping for hours. This missionary was watching all this and said to me, "What is it with all this stuff? It looks more demonic than godly to me." He couldn't understand it. I didn't know how to respond, so finally I said, "I'll tell you what. You seem sincere. Why don't we just pray for you?"
>
> So we prayed for him and asked the Lord to show him what was going on. Suddenly he flopped down on the ground and started rolling around like a bowling pin from one end of the stage to the other. He rolled into one wall, then rolled the other way into the other wall, saying "Ow" each time he hit a wall. He did this back and forth for some time. Finally he stopped, but couldn't walk on his own, so we carried him out. All he could say was "Wow!" I told him, "You have now set a new standard for all the skeptics." This missionary returned to his church in northern Russia and has subsequently sent us a couple of e-mails describing the healings and other miraculous things that have taken place in his church since he returned.

Passing the Anointing

Over the past year or so, life has been a whirlwind for the Stivers. They have ministered in Austria, Argentina, Slovakia, Chile, and Israel, as well as all over the United States. Everywhere they go they see the same evidences of God's Presence and anointing. They have learned to share what they have seen and to walk in the confidence that God will work through them. Rick explains:

Randy has been such a model for me because he is so normal. Whenever I see Randy doing something, I know there is hope for me. Recently, we were in a church in southern California, and I modeled what I had seen in Randy of asking the Lord to anoint people to pray. There were people there who needed prayer for sickness, so I asked the Lord to anoint people for prayer. About eight people in the audience felt like the Lord was anointing them to pray. They came forward and we anointed their heads with oil. As we did, God came and really shook them up. Most of these people had never seen or heard of anything like this before. One woman was a Baptist and she was wondering what was going on with this power coming over her. We had to guide her and tell her to pray for people. This is the kind of thing we have been seeing all over the world.

The exciting thing is the truth that all of us can now be a part of the Book of Acts. Seeing Randy do what he does has led me to believe that I can do it too, and that I can tell others that they can do it; we can all do the miraculous work for the

Lord. You don't have to be a full-time minister or a paid pastor to do the work of the Kingdom.

Strength Through Weakness

One of the things that Annie and Rick have learned is that when God uses us, more often than not, He uses us in our weaknesses and in areas we would never dream of, so that He gets the glory. Annie explains:

A few years ago, before all this happened, I had a big list of all my gifts, talents, and strengths. Yet God hasn't really used me in any of those areas, but in my weaknesses. One example is dance. When we visited Randy's church in St. Louis, DeAnne Clark prayed for me for dancing. Ever since then I have been released into an increasing ministry of dance before the Lord that is releasing others into a greater freedom of worship and in their relationships with Him. All my life I was a klutz. No matter what I did, I was clumsy. I tried out for track and broke my leg; I tried out for the modeling club and fell off the chair and ended up with my feet in the air; that kind of thing. Yet God has taken that and used it to bring Him glory and then to release others into their destiny in Him.

Rick adds:

Most of the ministry that God does with us now revolves around the dance. Annie never danced before she went to St. Louis and asked DeAnne to pray for her. She was on the floor after prayer, then got up some time later and went into almost a frenzy where she danced around for about five minutes until she fell exhausted to the floor. Since then she has danced all over the world and has collected flags and banners and hoops from all those places.

Open Doors

By the time this book is published, Rick and Annie and their family will have moved from their home of 20 years in California to a new home in Antioch, Tennessee, near Nashville. This is one of the latest ventures of faith in the exciting walk they have experienced since May 1995. As with their first trip to Russia, they do not know all that the Lord has in store in their move, but they are confident that He has everything in order. One possible connection is the burden they have for prayer and mission activity related to Israel; there are a number of prayer and intercession groups in Nashville praying for Israel.

Annie believes that God is in a season of preparing His Body:

He came and apprehended us to Himself and covered us with His blood, and in so doing brought healing to areas of our lives that we thought we had all together. Personally, we have had an apprehension of God by His love and healing and then we have gone out and taken it wherever He directs us, whether to people on the street or in the churches. God is looking for a people who will go when He says go, wherever He leads them.

Chapter 14

God Can Use
Little Ole Me

Grace was 12 years old; blonde, blue-eyed, beautiful—and blind. A rare disease had taken her eyesight when she was in kindergarten. I was in High Point, North Carolina, and she and two friends came up to me with such faith and expectation. We prayed for her and then I asked her if she could see anything. She said, "Yes, I think I can." She couldn't really, but she so wanted to believe! We prayed for her every session for three days. After the last one I asked her if she could see. She said, "No." Then I made a mistake. Emotion got ahead of wisdom and I reached down, hugged her, and whispered in her ear, "I'm so sorry you didn't get healed. I wanted you to see what a beautiful young woman you are becoming." She burst into tears, then reached over and grabbed her mom and just stood there, shaking and crying.

Fred Grewe witnessed this, and as I walked away with tears in my eyes he said, "She got behind your shield, didn't she?"

Why is it that so few Christians pray for the sick? It is not really a theological issue, despite the fact that a large segment of the evangelical Church has been taught that God does not heal anymore. Even within Pentecostal and Charismatic churches, who have a dynamic theology of healing, very few members pray for the sick with any consistency. The reason is emotional: praying for the sick is a heartrending ministry. There are both successes and failures in abundance. Not everyone who is prayed for gets healed, and that is painful. It is also reality.

The Agony of Defeat

Stunning success always carries the risk of devastating defeat. Athletes know this well. Repeated losses and failures must be endured before that first sweet victory comes. The old ABC television show *Wide World of Sports* had as its slogan, "The thrill of victory…the agony of defeat." We cannot experience the thrill of victory unless we are willing to embrace the agony of defeat.

I learned this early from John Wimber when I first got involved in praying for the sick. One night when he prayed, no one was healed. I said, "John, how can you live with that?" I'll never forget his answer. "Randy, it is not me when they get healed, and I don't take any credit for it. I am no different tonight than I was last night when several people got healed. I don't understand it. I am just willing to pray for the sick." What that meant to me was, "I'm willing to fail for Jesus." I said, "I can do that!" In the midst of my willingness to fail for Him, sometimes He will come and we'll see great healings take place. It's not us, but Him.

Often we do not pray for healing because we do not like pain and want to insulate ourselves from the suffering of others, yet part of being the Body of Christ means to identify with the cross. We must enter into Christ's suffering and be willing to enter into the pain of others. This kind of ministry invites failure, and we do not like to fail.

Another fear is what to say to someone who is not healed after prayer. Two things we should *never* say as stock answers are, "You didn't have enough faith," and "You must have sin in your life." The only truly honest answer we can give to the question, "Why wasn't I healed?" is to say, "I don't know." Why God heals sometimes and not others is a mystery. Paul said in First Corinthians, "For we know in part and we prophesy in part" (1 Cor. 13:9). Someday we will understand, but in the meantime we should exercise enough faith to pray for the sick.

By the way, Grace sent me a Christmas card that year, thanking me for praying for her. She said, "Don't give up. Keep praying for healing and I believe I will be healed." If Grace has the faith to believe in her healing, then I can have the faith to pray for her.

The Principle of Faith

There are five important scriptural principles for healing that work as principles, but backfire if we try to push them into rigid laws. The first of these is the principle of faith: "And without faith it is impossible to please God" (Heb. 11:6a); "According to your faith will it be done to you" (Mt. 9:29b); "Rise and go; your faith has made you well" (Lk. 17:19b). Faith is very important. In an atmosphere where there is much faith, much happens; where there is little faith, little happens.

The best biblical definition of faith is found in the Book of Hebrews: "Now faith is being sure of what we hope for and certain of what we do not see" (Heb. 11:1). I believe that, but I have another definition too:

> *Faith is not the absence of doubt;*
> *faith is facing the doubt and praying anyway.*

You see, I don't know when God is going to do it. I don't know when the person I lay hands on will suddenly feel the anointing in his body. I don't know who it is going to be. I have found out that it has little to do with me. My faith or lack of faith seems to have little bearing. Sometimes God sovereignly visits in spite of me. Yet I still prefer an atmosphere where there is a lot of faith. Then, in spite of the agonies of defeat, we can stand on the Word of God rather than on our experience and know that God will come.

Sometimes God heals despite a poor attitude. I was preaching a difficult series of meetings in Hendersonville, Tennessee. It seemed as though everything had gone wrong. One particular night I decided to preach to the young people rather than pray for the sick; the only night I was going to do that. As I was praying for them and God was touching them, a 49-year-old woman walked up to me. She looked like she was 60 and was shaking so much that she could hardly walk and had to be helped by her husband. At first I thought she was under the influence of the Holy Spirit, but it turned out she had Parkinson's disease. Her name was Anne Harrison; her husband's, Elvis.

I asked her what she wanted. She said, "I want you to pray for my healing." I said, "I'm not doing that tonight. I'm praying for the impartation. That's what God has on my heart." Anne said, "No, God told me that you were to pray for me." She had received a flier from the Baptist church that was hosting the meeting. She had never heard of Toronto or me. The flier mentioned that there had been healings in the meeting and as she had read it, she had heard the voice of the Lord in her spirit say, "Go to that meeting, have Randy pray for you, and I will heal you." When she told me that, I said I would pray for her, but I didn't expect anything.

My faith wasn't strong. I didn't even really want to do it; I was put out with her. I don't even think the prayer was very good. As soon as I began praying, though, she hit the floor and stopped shaking. Elvis told me it was normal for her to stop shaking when she was in a deep sleep. I thought she was in a deeper level of being slain in the Spirit. Anne had told me that she was facing a nursing home and did not want to live. She couldn't be a wife or a mother or hold her grandson because she shook so much. Her memory was going and she was losing control of her bowels and bladder. She had said, "If God does not heal me, I don't want to live anymore." That's when I finally reached out and touched her.

Elvis told me that Parkinson's attacked a particular area of the brain and destroyed the brain cells. Normally, there were 800,000 to 1,000,000 cells in the area affected, and Anne had only about 50,000 left. I told Elvis, "She needs a creative miracle, not healing!" I knelt down beside her and prayed, "Oh God, I call those things that are not as though they were. In the name of Jesus, I ask You for 800,000 new brain cells." When I said that she started moaning, "Stop praying, my head is killing me. Don't pray anymore." I never had a class at seminary that told me what to do in that situation, so I had to be led by the Spirit. I remember it as if it were yesterday. I said, "Oh God, don't listen to her prayer, listen to mine. More. More."

Instantly, Anne got as quiet as could be. All the pain was gone. So I said, "Anne, what's happening?" She said, "I don't feel anything." After lying on her back for a little while, Anne held her hand up to her face and just looked at it. It was as steady as a rock. Then she began holding her arms out to her sides and, one at a time, bringing them in to touch her nose with one finger. Elvis explained that this was a test for Parkinson's, and that Anne had not been able to do it for years. She asked for a drink of water, and got so excited when she was able to drink out of the cup. She had lost that ability too, and now she had it back.

We helped her up and she got up on the stage. She asked if we had a piano. We had a keyboard and she asked to play it. She played very well; another lost ability restored. Elvis said she had not been able to play for seven years. Then all of a sudden she began to sing Bill Gaither's song, "He Touched Me": "He touched me, oh, He touched me, and oh, the joy that floods my soul! Something happened, and now I know, He touched me and made me whole." There was not a dry eye in the place that night.

If I had been going by my faith, none of that would have happened. Because I acted on what little faith I had, the faith to pray, and went beyond doubt and fear, that gave God the opportunity to come in the name of Jesus. Faith is important, but keep it a principle. Don't turn it into a law.

The Principle of Sin

The second principle for healing is the principle of sin in one's life. Jesus healed the paralytic, then said, "Take heart, son; your sins are forgiven" (Mt. 9:2b). He told another person He healed to "stop sinning or something worse may happen to you" (Jn. 5:14b). The principle is that sometimes there can be some blockage by sin. For example, sometimes for arthritis there is the sin of bitterness, which must be renounced. Sometimes God will heal the person, but he or she must forgive in order to keep the healing. What happens when you turn that principle into a law? How much faith will you have that somebody will get healed if he is lukewarm? hypocritical? backslidden? unsaved? who is living in sin? If you turned the principle into a law, you will have no one healed. The law will boomerang and destroy your faith.

I remember a 25-year-old unsaved mother of two whom we found through a ministry of food for the poor at our church. She had a five-year-old daughter, a seven-year-old daughter, and an inoperable brain tumor. She couldn't handle chemotherapy and her doctor had advised her to prepare her will.

This young woman's previous live-in boyfriend had run off with all her money and emptied her checking account, leaving her destitute. She was totally un-churched and knew nothing about God. Two women from the church and I brought food to her and asked if we could pray for her. She said yes. I put my hands on her hair and the two women with me put their hands on her. We started praying and she said, "My head is getting hot." I said, "That's good." She looked at me and said, "You're weird." I assured her that I was not going to slap her or yell at her. We continued to pray and she said, "I feel electricity in my head and it is hot." I said, "That's good." She said, "You are *really* weird." Then she turned around and tried to talk to me. I was getting upset with her because she didn't know how to act. I was thinking, *God, she's not going to get healed. You're here and she's going to mess this up because of the way she is acting.* Then the Lord said, "Chill out, Randy. This one's on Me. Nothing is going to keep this one from happening."

Every two weeks for a month and a half we went and prayed for her. Then she called and said she didn't need any more help. It turned out that another boyfriend had moved in and she was ashamed for us to come. Several years later I ran into her at the food bank. I was amazed she was still alive. She told me that after we had prayed for her and she felt the electricity, she went to her doctor and the X-ray showed no cancer at all, only a concave opening where the brain hadn't filled in where that tumor had been. Then she said, "I always wondered if it had anything to do with when you prayed for me." I asked her if she would come to the church and share her story with our ministry team. Although she was still lost, she consented to come. As she gave the testimony of her healing, she broke down and cried when she remembered how she felt making out her will and having two young daughters. Sin in one's life is a principle, but don't turn it into a law.

The Principle of the Anointed Person

Do you believe there are some people who have a higher anointing than others? I do. There are those who have more of a gift, more of an anointing for healing than others. That's the principle of the anointed person. Even in the Bible there are times of greater and lesser healings. What if you don't feel like you are one of those anointed persons? What about the average "little ole me" in the church? Healing is not just for a select few people.

A friend of mine named Larry Randolph is a prophetic guy, and once when he was watching Benny Hinn, and saw the thousands of people in the auditorium, God spoke to him and asked, "What's wrong with that picture?" Larry said, "I don't know." The Lord said, "Benny needs competition." There is something wrong in the Church when there is so little healing that scores of thousands go where there *is* hope for healing. What He was saying is, "I want more people to believe that 'God can use little ole me.' "

Recently I received a letter from Great Britain containing a testimony of healing. On a previous visit, I had given a word of knowledge about Crohn's disease. The letter described how three people had been healed of Crohn's disease, one of whom had been scheduled for a colostomy the next day. The sister of a woman with the condition felt tremendous heat come into her stomach and colon, and she fell off her chair. The sister with Crohn's was not a believer. The sister who felt the heat called her mother and said, "Mum, I think God will heal her if she will come." She came. They had wanted me to pray with her, but for some reason I had missed her as I walked by. The woman who wrote the letter said that she had wanted to grab me and insist that I pray, but the Lord told her not to look to men for the healing. Then a teenaged girl from the local church came up and prayed for the sister with Crohn's. The power of God came on the woman and she was totally healed. The letter was written to encourage all the "little ole me's" to believe that God can touch them.

The Principle of the Anointing

The fourth principle is that of the anointing. All the time people come up to me and say, "Randy, what is it like when you feel the anointing?" To be honest, I usually don't feel anything. There are times when I have felt something, but that's not the norm. Some of the major healings have come when I didn't feel anything. If my faith is in feeling the anointing, I'm going to be discouraged because I don't feel it that often. My faith isn't in feeling, but in the Word that points me to Jesus, and in the promises of the Word. My faith is in Him, not in what I'm feeling. That's the principle of the anointing. There are times, though, when you do move in the anointing more strongly than at other times.

The Principle of Compassion

The fifth and final principle for healing is the principle of compassion. Moved with compassion, Jesus healed the sick. It's a good principle. We ought to pray, "God, I want to have Your compassion. I want to treat the people the way Jesus would treat them." Many people suffer periodically from "compassion fatigue": parents, pastors, evangelists; anyone who works in any kind of care-giving to people.

I was in Minneapolis, Minnesota. I had been gone for three weeks, I was missing my family, I was tired, I didn't feel good, and the meeting was a big responsibility. Most importantly, though, it had not been a real breakthrough meeting. I actually thought, *Oh God, I would like to just go home. Lord, I would like to lay here in bed and cover my head up. Lord, I don't want to go back out.* There were about 2,000 people there and I gave words of knowledge and said, "Everybody who wants to be prayed for to receive the blessing, go over to this side of the room." Fifteen hundred people stood up. Seventy-five percent of the ministry team went with them. I wanted to go over there. That was the fun side: fill, fill, fill. Five hundred people lined up for prayer related to the words of knowledge, and there was only a remnant of the ministry team. I looked at them and thought, *Oh God, I don't want to do this.* Now if I had turned the principle of compassion into a law, I would have felt disqualified: no faith, no expectation. How can God use someone who doesn't feel anything? How can He use someone who doesn't even want to pray for anyone? I started praying for the first person. Nothing happened. I prayed for the second person, and the third, and the fourth; nothing happened. That's a real faith builder!

The next person, an older gentleman, asked me to pray for the pain in his big toes. That did *not* go over well with me. Nevertheless, I knelt down, had him take his shoes and socks off, and I grabbed a big toe in each hand. I felt like I was milking a cow. I said, "In the name of Jesus, I command the pain to leave his big toes. In Jesus' name, I command the pain out of those big toes. Stop hurting. I command the pain to leave those big toes." All of a sudden the most terrible thought came into my mind. *I hope there is no one here who knows me. I look stupid and I sound stupid.* I wanted to quit so bad right then. So I went into my secret weapon: prayer. Only it's not the kind people can hear, but the kind only God can hear. *God, I don't want to be here. I feel terrible, I'm a total failure, and there is no anointing on me. I want to go home. God, why am I doing this? God, I want to quit.* In the middle of that honest prayer God gave me a mental image of my days growing up on a farm when, having fallen off a horse, I was told by my father to get right back up on it or else I would be afraid of it forever. God was telling me, "If you go to the house now, shame, guilt, and fear may take such a hold on you that you may never pray for the sick again." I knew what it meant. I said, "Lord, I'm not going to quit." So I went back to the normal prayer: "Big toe, in the name of Jesus, I command you to be healed!"

I finally made it over to the fun side, but I was pretty bummed out by that time. I sat down and a woman came up to me and said, "You look so tired, can I pray for you?" I said, "Sure." I had felt empty all night, but as she began to pray I felt a tingling starting over my head and going down my shoulders. I felt the Presence of God, and it was so good. When she finished I thanked her, and she asked me to pray for her. I thought it would be safe because she was over there on the fun side. I started to pray, "More," and she said, "No, I need healing." I asked her what was wrong. "I'm dying," she answered. "I have 28 cancers in my lungs, my lymph glands, and my neck."

I began to pray and instantly she said, "There is a tremendous heat going through my lung." I said, "Thank You, Jesus!" Was I any more anointed than I was earlier? Did I have more faith now than earlier? I don't know. I don't understand this thing; I just know how to recognize when the sovereign visitation for healing is present. She went to the doctors the next day and the tumors were gone from her lungs. I was so excited when she told me that the next night, but then she said, "I don't understand; I have two new ones over here." We prayed and they disappeared. The next night we prayed for her neck and shoulder area. The night we left, there was only one tumor remaining and it was the size of a pea.

Where was my compassion? If I had said I had to have compassion, I wouldn't have prayed that night. If I had to feel anointed, I wouldn't have prayed that night. Many of these tremendous miracles have occurred at some of my worst meetings.

How many people would you be willing to pray for and not see them healed, and still be willing to embrace the suffering of loving them and entering into their suffering? How many people would you be willing to pray for to see the blind eye open, to see a woman get her brain back, her memory back, or to see someone in severe pain healed? If you don't have the vision, if the goal is not before you, you will not be willing to pay the price.

Once, in my Baptist church, a 14-year-old spina bifida hydrocephalic girl was healed. She had already had 12 surgeries, one of which had cut some nerves, causing her to lose control of her bladder so she had to wear a diaper. When she was healed, it wasn't by any of the big-name guys; it was three women, a deacon, and myself praying for over 20 minutes. She got healed. Why would God do that? It is because He is committed to encouraging the Church to believe that "God can use little ole me." He can use little ole *you* too!

Other Books and Tapes

by Randy Clark and Global Awakening

BOOKLETS

God Can Use Little Ol' Me

Prophetic Foundations for Revival

Falling Under the Power of the Holy Spirit

The Baptism of the Holy Spirit

Learning How to Minister Under the Anointing

Cessation or Continuation of Spiritual Gifts

Unto Death—Freemasonry: Freedom in Christ or Bondage to Lucifer (by Barbara Cassada)

4-TAPE SERIES by Randy Clark
Heal the Sick

2-TAPE SERIES by Bill and Barbara Cassada
Understanding Demonization
(Deliverance Training)

To order materials or for information
about Global Awakening, contact:

Global Awakening
2923 Telegraph Road, St. Louis, MO 63125
Telephone: (314) 416-9239
Fax Number: (314) 416-7051
E-mail: goglobal@globalawakening.com
Website: http://www.globalawakening.com

CONFERENCE SERIES ON AUDIO CASSETTES

PRAYING DOWN THE FIRE

This conference trained the church to recognize and apply the vital relationship between effectual prayer and effectual evangelism. Speakers included Randy Clark; John Arnott, Senior Pastor of the Toronto Airport Christian Fellowship in Ontario, Canada; International Evangelist Mahesh Chavda; Jim and Ann Goll, founders of Ministry to the Nations; Jack Taylor, president of Dimension Ministries in Ft. Worth, Texas; Harold Caballeros, Senior Pastor of El Shaddai Church in Guatemala City, Guatemala; Gwen R. Shaw, founder of End-Time Handmaidens, Inc.; Rolland C. Smith, founder and international Director of Mission Omega.

CONQUERING THE CITY FOR GOD

"Setting the Captives Free" The Scriptures teach that this is a fundamental part of our ministry as disciples of Jesus. Before we can set others free, we must be free ourselves. Speakers are Dr. Pablo A. Deiros, Senior Pastor of "Del Centro" Evangelical Baptist Church, the oldest Baptist church in Argentina and second oldest in all of Latin America; Pablo Bottari, who is the General Coordinator of the Deliverance Ministry for Mensaje Salvacion, the evangelistic ministry of evangelist Carlos Annacondia; and Carlos Mraida, Pastor of "Del Centro" Evangelical Baptist Church in Buenos Aires.

(PROPHETIC SERIES)
WALKING IN THE PROPHETIC I, II & III
RAISING THE STANDARD

The purpose of these conferences was to learn what God is doing all over the world in the area of the prophetic. Each conference covered new material. Some of the topics covered are the Scriptural Basis for the Prophetic, Importance of the Prophetic in Today's Church, the Nature of Prophecy, Interpreting Dreams and Visions, Prophetic Etiquette, Prophetic Intercession, Prophetic Song, Women and the Prophetic, Prophetic Partnerships with Leaders. The speakers are Graham Cooke, Larry Randolph, Michael Sullivant, Jim and Ann Goll, Mike Bickle, James Ryle, John Paul Jackson, Mary Lindow, Dena Smith, and Randy Clark.

HEALING

This conference was designed to equip and empower God's people who have a passion to see His Kingdom advanced through physical healing. Speakers included Randy Clark; Larry Randolph, teacher and prophetic voice to the nations; Dr. Francis J. Sizer, a Roman Catholic priest; and Che Ahn, Senior Pastor of Vineyard Christian Fellowship of Greater Pasadena.

All of the above are available from:
GLOBAL AWAKENING
2923 Telegraph Rd., St. Louis, MO 63125
Tel: (314) 416-9239   Fax: (314) 416-7051

Exciting videos
by Randy Clark

GOD CAN USE LITTLE OLE ME

Many believe that God can heal, but often there is no ongoing healing ministry by the laity in their local church. If you want to be effective in a healing ministry, or if you've ever needed encouragement to pray for the sick, then this message is for you. Learn how to pray in obedience to God's Word, and then watch little faith blossom into big faith as God begins to move!
ISBN 0-7684-0056-2 Retail $14.99

MAKING OF A MIGHTY WARRIOR

The call of God always comes with a promise. But as Randy Clark shows from the life of Gideon, there is always a process of crises that believers must go through in order to reach the fulfillment of that promise. This process is the path that God's chosen ones must walk through to become the mighty warriors that He has called them to be. The conflict we encounter in crises leads us to the place of prayer. There faith comes and enables us to walk as warriors with power.
ISBN 0-7684-0055-4 Retail $14.99

OUT OF THE BUNKHOUSE

What is God's heart for the historical liturgical Church, as well as for the New Wavers, the Charismatics, and others? With fresh insight and revelation, Randy gives us a perspective from the story of the Prodigal Son that will touch your heart and perhaps change any long-standing attitudes about God's newer additions to His Church. You'll find yourself examining your attitudes and perspectives as you learn of the place you have in your Father's House.
ISBN 0-7684-0060-0 Retail $14.99

YOU'VE GOT TO SERVE SOMEBODY

ISBN 0-7684-0089-9 Retail $14.99

Available at your local Christian bookstore.

Internet: http://www.reapernet.com

Other *Destiny Image titles*
you will enjoy reading

THE POWER OF BROKENNESS
by Don Nori.
Accepting Brokenness is a must for becoming a true vessel of the Lord, and is a step-ping-stone to revival in our hearts, our homes, and our churches. Brokenness alone brings us to the wonderful revelation of how deep and great our Lord's mercy really is. Join this companion who leads us through the darkest of nights. Discover the *Power of Brokenness*.
ISBN 1-56043-178-4 $9.99p

THE LOST ART OF INTERCESSION
by Jim W. Goll.
The founder of Ministry to the Nations, Jim Goll has traveled the world in a teaching and prophetic ministry. All over the globe God is moving—He is responding to the prayers of His people. Here Jim Goll teaches the lessons learned by the Moravians during their 100-year prayer Watch. They sent up prayers; God send down His power. Through Scripture, the Moravian example, and his own prayer life, Jim Goll proves that "what goes up must come down."
ISBN 1-56043-697-2 $9.99p

ENCOUNTERS WITH A SUPERNATURAL GOD
by Jim and Michal Ann Goll.
The Golls know that angels are real. They have firsthand experience with supernatur-al angelic encounters. In this book you'll read and learn about angels and supernatur-al manifestations of God's Presence—and the real encounters that both Jim and Michal Ann have had! As the founders of Ministry to the Nations in Antioch, Tennessee, and speakers and teachers, they share that God wants to be intimate friends with His people. Go on an adventure with Jim and Michal Ann and find out if God has a supernatural encounter for you!
ISBN 1-56043-199-7 $9.99p

USER FRIENDLY PROPHECY
by Larry J. Randolph.
Hey! Now you can learn the basics of prophecy and how to prophesy in a book that's written for you! Larry J. Randolph, a favorite speaker for prophetic and renewal con-ferences throughout the world, began to function as a prophetic voice to the nations at the age of 23. Whether you're a novice or a seasoned believer, his book will stir up the prophetic gift God placed inside you and encourage you to step out in it.
ISBN 1-56043-695-6 $9.99p

Available at your local Christian bookstore.

Internet: http://www.reapernet.com